THE MANY FACES OF

EMMA CURTIS HOPKINS
1849-1925

1885

1891

Esoteric Philosophy

Deeper Teachings in Spiritual Science

Emma Curtis Hopkins

Esoteric Philosophy: Deeper Teachings in Spiritual Science
By Emma Curtis Hopkins
© WiseWoman Press 2011

Managing Editor: Michael Terranova

Vancouver, Washington

www.wisewomanpress.com

ISBN: 978-0945385-2-19

CONTENTS

FOREWORD i
LESSON   I 1
LESSON   II 7
LESSON   III 15
LESSON   IV 21
LESSON V 33
LESSON   VI 41
LESSON   VII 53
LESSON   VIII 59
LESSON   IX 67
LESSON   X 72
LESSON   XI 79
LESSON   XII 84

FOREWORD

The operations of nature are the clothing of man's will. The operations of destiny are the clothing of his mind. The experiences of freedom from nature and destiny are the clothing of his soul. And his soul folds him around with its still more profound mystery.—*ech*[1]

From the late 1880s through the beginning of the 20th century Emma Curtis Hopkins taught thousands of people to become healers, including the founders of Unity, Religious Science, and Divine Science. Her initial twelve lessons were based on Mary Baker Eddy's teachings and were a very effective way to learn how to heal oneself and others, and to teach those others how to heal, as well. Over time and with study, however, those initial lessons were modified and became her own.

The new teachings introduced a new way of thinking and being. They offered a line of reasoning that brought her students out of the habit of "blind faith" into a powerful, logic-based "understanding faith" that could not be undermined by any circumstance.

As she taught, practiced, and worked with these ideas, however, Emma herself began to find a new level of understanding. She began to see that the state of mind and feelings that led to healing was desirable in itself. She began to move from trying to make things happen in her life and world to simply being in that state of connection with the divine.

---

[1] From this book, *Esoteric Philosophy*, p. 23,

As her students observed the change, they asked to know more, and so Emma, ever the loving teacher, created a series of lectures for those few who could move beyond the surface and into the depths. For a wider audience, she pulled her lectures together in a book, entitled *High Mysticism,* which is now published by WiseWoman Press. But for the few, these teachings were passed on as mimeographed sheets from one hand to another until Marge Flotron of Chicago had a few copies printed.

It's from these few copies that the following text is taken. Virtually no editing has been done to Ms. Flotron's version, except to clarify footnotes and references.

LESSON I

In metaphysics there is always what is said, and underneath what is said is what is implied. For *meta* means beyond, and beyond need have no limit. We are not limited in mental range. The ideal is able to stretch itself into the very core of things where they had their origin. Did not Boehme[2] stretch his ideals into the Abysmal Dark which was before even God began?

The penetrative sense of mind is its freeing sense. Without exercising its penetrative sense, mind imprisons itself in matter and sleeps. It is not content with matter. Bodies languish and enter graves because the mind has not penetrated through bodies, through things and objects with a strong sense of things not seen. When mind flies beyond words, when it dives below words, when it wings itself on strong pinions independent of words, it carries the molecules of bodies into light and living transfigurations.

There is a Science of sciences. It is the philosophy that mind spreads its senses over matter while words are being spoken. Hamilton, the Scotch metaphysician, called this philosophy the Science of the Absolute indifference of the ideal and the real. How indifferent to the seeming is the esoteric sense, the wordless sense and touch of mind when it lets itself loose from matter. The first lesson in the esoteric of His dogma was given by Jesus Christ in this text:

---

[2] Jacob Boehme (1575-1624), Christian mystic and author of *The Way to Christ* and *The Signature of All Things*.

"The Lord said unto my Lord, sit Thou on My right hand till I make thine enemies thy footstool." [Psalms 110:1]

The Lord that speaks to my Lord is the Highest Brahman or Undescribed God, the First and Uncompanioned One. My Lord is my Ego or Reason. My Ego or Reason, with its sense of hearing so unlike my ears with their tympanum, hears in its own fashion, and it translates what it hears into common language. It puts what it hears from the Highest Brahman into words. It tells my tongue to speak on one side only till I see death, material limitations, misery, ignorance, slip under my feet and I see myself standing upright as Jesus saying one moment in final certainty, "I have overcome the world."

The side that my tongue (the instrument of my Ego when it would sound itself on matter), must speak, is that on the side where the mind is looking, there is only Good. The Good is omnipresent, omnipotent, omniscient. The Good reigns. The Good is God. The Good is Life. Life reigns on the right side where I turn my mind. The Good is Truth. Truth reigns on the right side where I turn my mind. The Good is Love. Love reigns on the right side where I turn my mind. It will sit on this side in judgment. That is my mind. It shall judge in all things, in all discussions, that the Good shall reign. And the Good shall always come off victorious. If man tells me that evil reigns, my judgment shall sit still while its tongue tells its irresistible Truth. The irresistible Truth shall ever be that the Good is there where the evil seems to be and shall reign instead of evil.

All wrong shall fail when my reasoning sits in judgment saying, that because the Good is God, it cannot be overthrown. The white stone of Revelation is the Good that stays fixed eternally in the universe and reigns. Whoever sees the Good that is fixed in the universe sees the white stone. Whoever sees that the Good cannot be defeated, will have it revealed unto him that even while he is thus seeing the undefeatableness of the Good, the world around him shall see it also. For his mental sense is strong, it is pungent, it is awakening. It carries even the outer senses on its wings.

Whoever sees that the Truth is God, will tell the Truth and it will defeat every lie. The Truth concerning the Good is the only Truth. The man who accuses me of wrong thoughts or wrong actions tells not the Truth. The only Truth he could speak concerning me would be of the fixed Good that is in me. If I took his purse, he shall not see theft; he shall see the fixed Good in me. So the Highest Lord tells me to see the fixed Good in my enemies and they will have no power to hurt me. The Highest Lord tells me to see the fixed Good in the action of the thief and that fixed Good will reveal itself even to him. He cannot help changing from thieving to kindness to his neighbors when I see the fixed Good.

The ability to sit on the right side is the ability that even the child has by native trend. The child believes in the beauty and kindness of the asp and the crocodile till it is told they are neither beautiful nor kind. The child who keeps his mind on the original idea he brought from heaven, will be the Jesus Christ child.

The man who restores unto himself the idea of beauty and kindness inherent in all things, will restore himself to his former glory that he had with the Father before the world appeared unto him. He has nothing to do in putting evil, matter, pain, death off the earth: he has only to sit on the right hand of all things, all people, all principle, till the Lord put all death and pain under his feet for him. Man has to insist on the fixed Good in the anarchist. He has to insist on the fixed Good in the capitalist. He thus watches the white stone of revealing. One thing after another will drop under his feet without his personal effort: yea, even without his mental effort; yea, even without his sight or feeling being touched.

"In the stone a new name: and I will give him to eat of the hidden manna." [Revelation 2:17] The promised manna of life is the unspeakable kindness of the Lord whose undescribed presence talks in its own wondrous language to my Lord, or my talking and moving Ego, my human mind at its highest intelligence.

The first lesson to man was given many times over by Jesus, sometimes simply, sometimes abstrusely, yet always with esoteric implyings farther and farther than the ego can tell until it has sat on the side of the Good, has seen the fixed Good in all things, not with his outer eyes, not with his heart, but with his principles,

He has not spoken aloud to the poverty-stricken wretch crying with hunger; but silently, with his reasoning, he has said unto his mind, "Because the Good is God, because God the Good is kind and bountiful, thou art not hungry." This manner of secret reasoning conveys a white, fine food to the mind which has the power to turn into bread the money to buy meat and milk for the howling wretch.

The unemployed masses must have someone to sit on the right side in principle in mind till the Good that is God takes them out of inferiority and makes them equals with kings and princes in possessions and opportunities brought forward by the steady right reasoning of some one man or woman who will not agree that their want and ignominy are reality; for the Good that is God is loving kindness and is not partial to princes and kings, leaving the poor in cold neglect.

Mary, sitting still and declaring this, shall see it everywhere. She shall convert the world. Martha, trying to make Mary see how hard life is, how slow the Good is, shall not reign. Her evil declarations shall not stand. Her estimates shall not abide. They shall fall into nothingness.

God is a providing goodness. The red of the rose is not more sure than Mary's food and beauty. So the everlasting principle of power shall reign in the sight of all men. It is the native notion of the Lord of life, health, strength, support, protection, intelligence, beauty, power, when my Lord proclaims the first lesson of Jesus in esoteric philosophy.

One of his first lessons to man was expressed in the words: "Repent, for the Kingdom of God is at hand." [Mathew 3:2] "The Kingdom of heaven is within you." "Pray unto your Father in heaven." [Luke 11:2] See how, by the philosophy of the Absolute, He here teaches man to pray unto his own Self. See how, by this lesson, He shows that the Lord, the Highest Brahman, the Father, the First One, is in all men alike. To their own God within themselves, to the highest of themselves, they shall address themselves: "Give me this day, my daily supply." [Luke 11:3] Let me not walk on the side of the hard and the unkind appearance, even when to my eyes and heart it seems so real. "Thou art my light and my life. Thou art my salvation. Great art Thou, having Thy everlasting presence even in me, ever near for me to call upon. I fear no evil, for Thou art with me."

Repentance is turning from expecting some external being to come down and do for us. Repentance is turning to the "I AM," the God, the Lord, the Father at our own center, and reasoning from its presence in us in its glory to its glory in all the earth. "Because I am, thou art." Repentance is turning from judging your life and character by the human and lying aside. It is judging it by the divine and eternal side.

The fixed Good will seem to work swiftly if I see it with my heart's conviction while I am obeying the simple direction of talking and thinking about the fixed Good, regardless of externals. He who speaks of the fixed Good, is translating from the Lord's instructions into my Lord's speech.

He who sits in that judgment concerning me will behold that I am God at my center. I who hear His voice, turn to behold my God. I am satisfied with myself. I am happy in myself. I behold that my own Highest Brahman is the Lord. I behold not any more human nature. Thus repenting, I take the manna of beholding God, the Lord, everywhere. To me all is God.

LESSON II

The Statement of Being, which is the title of the first lesson in metaphysics, conveys the inspiration to mind, as a wind might blow into our nostrils, that there is conflict now going on between two powers: Good and evil; Spirit and matter; Life and death; and that in the conflict, Spirit will prevail, and after the smoke of battle has cleared away, we shall see that all is Spirit, for Spirit is ever victorious when pitted against matter.

Every first lesson in metaphysics conveys this breath inward upon us. It is the inspiration or inbreathing of doctrine. But the mind is like the body in that its expiration is as important as its inspiration. The second lesson of metaphysics, or mind, is expiration. It is the throwing off or refusal of what is not vital. It is not a Truth that there is conflict between two substances, Spirit and matter, although matter is dissolved at once by presenting Spirit before it. "The earth is clean dissolved before us, saith the Lord." [Isaiah 24:19]

In heeding the injunction of Jesus Christ to sit on the right hand, we call God, Spirit. We call God, Life. We call God, Truth. We call God, Love. Thus we are seeing Life everywhere and ignoring death. We are breathing forth from our mind, its ideas not essential.

The only death there is, then, is letting go our idea of death. The idea of death is not essential to Life. There is no conflict between death and Life. The only death of hate or ignorance there can be is letting go our ideas of hate and ignorance. The idea of hate is not vital. It is not essential. The idea of ignorance is not vital. It is not essential. So, in the breath of mind outward, we let go of ideas and this is their death.

Jesus Christ said to John, "I am He that liveth and was dead, was dead and am alive forevermore." [Revelation 1:18] He spoke then of how the Jews had tried to breathe Him away from their mind; while being the vital Truth, he could not be lost but must live forevermore.

There is a presence of Jesus Christ within us, breathed through the mind by His name, which shows us that the Life that is God may quicken us into a state which has no opposite to be sent forth from our mind. There is a Life beyond the life that has to let go of death. By breathing into the nostrils the atmosphere and at the same time drawing into the mind the name Jesus Christ, we are taking in both mental and physical breaths. That name has in it a quickening energy. It expels the money changers or our sordid notions, by its mystic body which is now within us when we inspire it.

There is a life that knows no death. It is the Jesus Christ Life. The mystery of it is the state it brings us into, by breathing the name "Jesus Christ" "The Holy Spirit whom the Father will send in My Name."

There is an intelligence that knows no ignorance. It is that Intelligence we breathe into our mind by drawing into it the mystic Body of Jesus Christ by the Name.

There is a Love that is beyond letting go of hate. It is the Love which inspires those who inspire, as a breath, the Name Jesus Christ. "Your joy no man taketh from you."

The Statement of Being, or first lesson in Good as Mind, as Intelligence, tells us of Omnipresent,

Omnipotent Omniscient Life. It asks us to read from the page of our own idea of Good in Life and say that there is no death in our idea of Good. It asks us to read from the page of our idea of Substance and say that it must be unfailing Presence.

It is a Science which casts out evil, matter, sickness, death, hate, error, sin. It is a Science of establishing the Kingdom of Spirit by proclaiming that all is Spirit, there is no matter; all is Life, there is no death. It is a Science which never feels the inspiration of conflict. Whereas, there is a Science of expiration of the breath of conflict. It is the Science of death, "I am He that was dead." It is the Substance which enters the body when mind breathes in the Name Jesus Christ. Ideas of death are gone. Ideas of ignorance are gone.

What were they? They were Jesus Christ in an esoteric sense. Who is the death of our former body and former mind so absolutely as He whose Name puts mind and body both out of consciousness forever and occupies them Himself? Who is so wise as He who knows a state untouched by evil and Good? This is Jesus Christ.

Our very ideas of ignorance and death are Jesus Christ. The Science of denials leads us to see that when we say there is no evil, all is Good, we are putting out Jesus Christ and retaining Jesus Christ. For the evil which we refuse is, in its esoteric or mystic sense, the ministry of destruction. There is no destroyer like Jesus Christ. "I came not to bring peace on earth, but a sword." [Matthew 10:34]

But it is not vital, it is not essential, to look upon evil and death as Good. It is vital still to say they do not exist. It is vital to say that there is no conflict between Spirit and matter, for Spirit is all when speaking of these two. For in Christian preaching, we sit on the side of Spirit and Life. Yet

Jesus Christ said, "Blessed are the poor in Spirit, for theirs is the Kingdom." [Matthew 5:3] He saw that in Himself there were no pairs of opposites. He saw that Himself once being breathed into your body and mind through inspiring His Name, you would, like Him, see with your mystic body that Spirit, being one of a pair of opposites, is now melted and gone like its opposite, matter.

It is utter poverty of Spirit to be as free from Spirit as from matter. He called it blessedness. It is constant preaching of all is Good, there is no evil, which brings Good into view as the victorious, in metaphysics. It is constant preaching of all is Spirit, there is no matter, which brings Spirit into view as the victorious doctrine, in metaphysics. It there stops, and Jesus Christ takes the reins of mind exactly as promised, "I will make thine enemies thy footstool." [Psalms 110:1]

It is the "I" at the center which is exposed by breathing in the doctrine of all is Good and breathing out the doctrine that there is no evil. Both statements are true. One swings the curtain of human experience to the right from the center, the other parts it to the left. There stands the exposed center. One breathes the breath of Truth inward, and the other breathes it outward.

The one who breathes the statements is ever independent of them all. Is not the man more important than his breath? Set free from his breaths, is he not something which is neither inspiration nor expiration?

That which is independent is the state of mind exactly identified or identical with the One who can lay down His breath and take it up again at will. What name stands for that Being? So then, he who can lay down his breaths and pick them up again at will, is the Jesus Christ man.

Physically, we are told that the breath is the life of man. By the knowledge of the Jesus Christ body through Spiritual Science, we perceive that there is a Life independent of the physical. It is the metaphysical. On this point, Jesus Christ says, 'The flesh profiteth nothing. My words are Spirit and Life." [John 6:63]

Then further, the words of mind which Jesus Christ and all the prophets [being, as you understand, twelve in number], taught, cause you — when you use them — to be independent of words.

When we see how our true body, or our true "I," standing back and breathing in the names of God and describing His place, power and wisdom, and breathing outward the rejection of all that is not God, is, after all, only using words exactly as it uses breaths, we realize that indeed something is more wonderful than words.

What is it? It is the "I" that uses them. Here we say with Jesus Christ, this "I" is the Father or First Mover of the breath of the physical body as air, and the breath of mind as words or ideas. The "I" fathers all things, that is, it starts all things. It is the mystic body of all men alike. Whoever gets back of breaths and back of thoughts to his majestic starting point, is one with Jesus Christ indeed. He knows that he is himself and God in one. Yet he is neither life nor death.

As the state which is not life, but which causes life, we see that we may also be the cause of death. "I can lay down my body and I can take it up again," [John 10:17] said Jesus Christ, referring to His handling of His outward garment of man and His hidden garment of mind.

Laying down the book you are reading seems to destroy information. Taking it up seems to revive its information. If the body that is sustained by inspiration and expiration of wind is but an appearance, is it not easy to lay it off for Him who stands back folding it around Himself? If the body, more metaphysical, which we call the mind, is but an appearance sustained by the wind of thoughts that come and go, is it not easy for the One that stands back and wraps the mind around Himself, to lay it off and pick it up again?

The statement that Jesus Christ is the evil that we say has no reality, is sometimes called the only difficult statement.

Do you think it difficult to say that Jesus Christ or the "I" back of your mind must be that which stops the breath and sets it going again? Do you think it difficult to say that the "I" that stands back must be the one who stops thoughts and sets them going? When a breath stops breathing, we call it death. It is certainly the "I" back of the breath that stopped it. If we breathe inward the Name Jesus Christ and hold the breath and then let it go, we find at the fountain-head of our being a body not mixed up with the breath at all.

All the evil sights and sounds of our daily observation are the stopping of thoughts by our own "I." Let the thoughts go freely forth again and see what a change of appearance will result. Suppose a man strikes a horse. It is the "I" of yourself stopping the thought of peace. Let the thought go free again and see how peaceful the horse will feel, how peaceful the man will feel, how still the whip will lie.

Do you wonder that in the doctrine of Christian Mental Practice we have the reasonable idea that there is no pain, no discord? The simple denial of pain and discord is Truth. The understanding that the mystic "I" back of all thoughts stops them and starts them, explains why there is no pain, no discord. This "I" is again fed at its own fountain-head by its own Lord, and when we keep to the doctrine that all is Good, there is no evil, we are touching the "I" at our center, who breathes and thinks. We hear our own "I" or self taking its breath of inspiration from its Lord.

The Brahmins taught that only the "Self" can know the "Self." The words of Jesus were, "The Lord saith unto my Lord, 'Who is "The Lord?"'" It is the Absolute Self who feeds "my Lord." Who is "my Lord"? It is the "I" at my center who breathes and thinks but is always something independent of breaths and ideas. The "I" at my center is my "Self." That which the Brahmins said this "Self" might become acquainted with is its "Self" upon whom it depends, upon whom it feeds. When the independent "I" sits on the right of its "Lord," it says, "All is God." It says, "That which is not God does not exist."

Nourished by these two breaths, the religions of all ages have declared that man shall live as God forever. He may lay off his life forever. He may "rest from his labors of thoughts and his works shall follow him."

Whoever sees God sees his own "Self." Whoever sees God, is God. Whoever sees God performs the works of God. Wherever he breathes his breaths, Good appears. Wherever he thinks his thoughts, Good appears. He knows that whatsoever seems evil is only his breath drawn inward. Letting his breath go free again, peace and joy and light and life are shed forth on its wings.

He knows that whatsoever seems evil is only his thoughts gathering in upon himself. Letting them go again freely, over the earth, he sees light, joy, peace, intelligence, shedding themselves on their wings. He sees that he is Lord over all the earth. He sees that the denials of Science have a reason for themselves in the fact that he is as the "I" at the center is that God who breathes into the creature's breath of life, or withdraws breath — at free choice. Looking toward his God transcending himself, he sees only God and he never sees less than God.

LESSON III

"There shall be no more caterpillar" is prophesied for the days when man has embodied himself by eating his own substance. Why is there such an appearance of hunger everywhere? Is not everything longing and gnawing to fill itself with something different from what it has already on hand? This is its caterpillar state. It must ever be gnawing till it strikes its native body. Can anyone suppose that the Almighty God is gnawing after more food than He already has? So if my body is gnawing to make more substance for itself, then both my mind and my body are in the caterpillar condition, and the day of God is not known to me even though I am preaching great doctrine and making myself famous for great knowledge of God.

The eating practice of the body is called "feeding." The eating practice of the mind is called "affirmation." Both affirmation and feeding are wholly ungodly. The Lord sits in the heavens and laughs afar out of the reach of the calamities that come from eating. And the day when I cease from affirmation, that day I am the Lord and I am far out of the reach of calamity to mind. And that day when my body ceases from eating, the body of the Lord is presented alone.

"I will restore to you the years that the caterpillar [locusts] hath eaten," saith the Lord. [Joel 2:25] This is the fact. I lose no time by eating, I lose no time by thinking, I lose no Lordship by feeding a body of flesh though I should spend a million years feeding myself. I lose no Godhead by thinking and thinking, though I should spend a million years thinking. For the years which the caterpillar hath eaten are suddenly restored, no matter what I have done or said or thought. Restoration cannot take place where something is lost. The very word "restoration" shows that the something was always somewhere to be laid hold of. So nothing is ever lost, nothing is ever gained, in fact. He who lives in fact said plainly, "Nothing can be added to, or taken from, the "I". Therefore, nothing said against any man gives him any hurt. Nothing said for a man, gives him any good. He is what he is; he always was what he is; He always will be what he is. This is Almighty God, untouchable, unhinderable.

If the world of matter fights, it is fighting for this God. So God is the innocent cause of all the fighting. Man gnaws to be satisfied and undestroyable, like the Almighty "I" but as the Almighty "I" never gnaws to get Himself undestroyable, it is plain that gnawing by fighting will not find the satisfied "I" any more than gnawing by eating or affirming.

The wisest of mankind have believed that in rest of some sort they should be satisfied. They have known that pure rest is pure God. Yet they have still kept on urging their minds and bodies to do things to find God. Their very rest has been self-torturing. Their very principle of thoughts has been self-tormenting, and as all torturing has been caterpillar effort, it is plain that man's rest is not God's rest till there is no torturing about it.

Solomon proclaimed that there never had been anything new and there never would be anything new. This is Truth. That which is, already is all there is of us. We cannot change in fact. The Lord restores what we have supposed we had lost and, lo, it is now as it already was. In the various sciences, men are gnawing to discover that which already exists and work it over into combinations which already exist somewhere. In the Science of Christ, we are laying hold upon life which already exists in essence and in manifest. We say that man has all the life there is. We lay hold upon a health which already exists and we say that man already owns all the health there is. We say we lay hold upon strength which already exists, and we say man already owns all the strength there is.

Then to be seeking life, health, strength, peace, is to be gnawing after what we already have. "The press is full, the vats overflow," said Joel. [Joel 3:13] It is reasonable to conclude that if all that man is seeking is already in his possession, he would better stop seeking and rest in ownership.

In the Scriptures, the Name of the "I AM" is synonymous with His presence—and power. "Thy Name is an ointment poured forth." [Song of Solomon 1:3] "The Name of the Lord is a strong tower." [Proverbs 16:10] Do we know anyone with the pronunciation of the Lord on his lips so that the ointments are poured forth on him? Do we know anyone already showing forth that he is a strong tower? How the children shouted hosannas to Jesus because He knew the Name of the Lord. They never sang about His feeding the hungry or healing the sick. The Name of the Lord is in every man. He need not go seeking after it. Every man is entrenched in an unscalable tower of eternal safety, who owns a name that saves.

Many years ago in India lived a man whose name spoken by anyone in danger, would save him promptly. Soon his name lost its safety. The Name of the Lord is eternal ointment, eternal safety. No man can tell that Name, for telling it supposes hunger to do something. So man keeps the saving Name of the Lord unspoken, untold, unthought. He keeps it where he is not hungry. Let not man suppose that by feeding his body with sufferings he shall find the unhungry Lord-Name which he already owns.

Simeon of Antioch perched on one tower 60 feet high for 37 years. An iron chain about his neck caused his forehead to touch his feet. His caterpillar nature hungered for suffering to appease its deeper hunger. As this amount of suffering did not satisfy, he added further tortures. He took only two meals per week. This is asceticism of body trying to find the "I" which needs nothing. It does not spiritualize this caterpillar performance to call it *hatha yoga* philosophy. It has been practiced thousands of years without adding to the knowledge and power of the ever-satisfied, unhungry God.

When a man talks of certain actions which he must not perform and of certain actions which he must perform, he is a hungering caterpillar seeking God by *hatha yoga.*

When a man tells of certain thoughts which he must spin around and of certain ones which he must never think, he is a caterpillar on the mental plane, hungering after his unhungry "I" by gnawing thoughts* He does not make this gnawing more divine by calling it *raja yoga* philosophy. Yet one thing is done with the hungry body feeding it, viz., it is worn out; and one thing is done with the hungry mind also, viz., it is worn out with the excitement of thoughts; therefore, both mind and body are temporal, unreal, while the majestic Original Me is eternal Substance.

The Original Me, the eternal "I" Substance," is by itself, not identified with anything, yet is the eternal cause of all, as the sun is the cause of the grass, yet is never identified with the grass. As the grass looks toward the sun, it becomes more and more beautiful as grass till it finally is lost in sunshine.

The body and mind with their hungry gnawings turn to look at the divine Me, and it shines so wondrously through them that they are beautiful. They turn even to transfiguration. The look of the body toward the Original Me, beautifies it. There is a power of the very eyeballs to turn up and back, which is transfiguring. There is a way of inner eyesight, the mind's eye turning backward and upward toward the Original Me, till it never has to speak or think for itself, for the original unhungry, shining Me streams in radiance through it till there is no mind whatever.

"The Lord is not slack concerning His promises," said Peter. [2 Peter 3:9] This is true, for the moment we turn the hungry eyeballs toward the throne, the Lamb that sits thereon leads and feeds with himself in the fullness of glory, so that there is no hungry body left. The inflow of the Lamb glory is instantaneous, as when a pent-up fire rushes through a draught, or as when the focused sun rays kindle on a pine board.

"Look unto Me and be ye saved, all the ends of the earth." [Isaiah 45:22] The mind's eye can turn to that Lamb on the throne with the Name that cannot be spoken. Suddenly, down through that open door, the unspeakable glory descends, and the unhungry God fills the house.

The inspiration of the Lamb is its own fiery nature. The earth that gnaws shall be filled with that nature, that glory, that inspiration. It is not by gnawing and eating, but by turning and looking.

The most heavily weighted mind may turn and look. All its weights are gone; all the Lamb's inspiration wings its splendor through it. Rahab[3] was a harlot, but she knew her own divinity once and it so beautified her enemies that she called them divine. So they befriended her and she gave birth after a few generations to Jesus, the inspired. The cripple at the gate had seen his own Lamb on his own throne, his Original Me, and then Peter and John looked omnipotent in his eyes.

"For what thou seest, man,

That, too, become thou must;

And around about thy life,

The way be God, or dust."

The hunger of the eyes to see is sign of there being something to see, which, being seen, is all that remains. The hunger of the ears to hear is sign of there being something to hear, which being heard, that is all that there is of us. The hunger of the hands to touch and the tongue to taste is sign of there being an Original Me to touch and taste, and, when they have thus tasted, there is nothing of them but It.

Back of all the hungry senses is their Substance.

They make themselves open doors wide as God, and those doors can be no more shut forever.

Turn ye — turn ye — why play the caterpillar when the Almighty God is bread!

---

[3] Rahab: A woman of Jericho who aided the two spies that Joshua sent there and aided them in getting away safely. For this act, she and her family were saved when the Israelites took the town. DAVID and JESUS were descended from her. [Joshua 2:1-24; 6:23-25; Ruth 4:21].

LESSON IV

The Adam man names good and evil.

The Joshua man names good only. The Christ man names neither good nor evil.

The Adam man speaks from common sense and with fair reasoning from the merits of the question of easy and difficult, sick and well. The Joshua man finds only grapes of Eschol on the plains where Adam shows you plainly that giants of terror abide with menacing fronts. The Christ man ignores the grapes of Eschol and the giants of difficulty. He knows that good and evil are only clothes which man may put on or leave off. This is Christ Jesus in truth, namely, that which is in the world but not of it.

While I am sleeping I am in the midst of my mystic garment; but am I the garment we call sleep? While I dream, am I not aware forever that all that happens, happens unto me and I am never that which happens? If it seems close, do I not still feel that, though in the dream, I am not of it?

What is this me that is never anything that happens? What is this which is able to leave the panorama of every transaction behind me and draw it aside from me, no matter how much attention I have given it? Does my attention unto a thing make me that thing? Plato says, "That thou seest, that thou beest," but every man, woman and child in the universe knows that he is not that which he sees. Everyone knows that what he sees is something folded around him and is no more himself than the sun was the woman that John, the Revelator, saw. When

Charcot[4] whispers to me that an onion is an orange, what is that of me which agrees with Charcot and what is that of me which sits in a serene independence of Charcot? What is the Me?

All lessons of metaphysics drive to one and one only. Notice those denials and affirmations we have gathered from the thoughts of Christian Science found in Science and Health and repeated from the books of the sages of all ages. They are every one calculated to draw us more and more closely to inquiry into who and what the body of knowledge beyond knowledge may be. If I tell of the ascetics of bygone times struggling to see this unnamed and unmoved self, I am telling of their experiments that I may avoid their unprofitable ones and experience whatever they tell in their books they have discovered that is able to clothe and unclothe them, of that which is not their Self.

Perhaps the whole metaphysics of all times might be driven down to the operation of clothing and unclothing that unseen Self. It is evident that no mystic of mighty doctrine ever did any more than wrap himself with new experiences which he called soul or mind or Spirit sensations. Is not a man something free and superior to his senses? Am I not superior to my clothes? Even if I make my clothes my chief in life, I care more for myself than I do for my clothes, for it is for myself I clothe myself. Therefore, the sages of China, of Arabia, of India, of Egypt, were yet superior to and different from their experiences of Soul.

The doctrine of concentrating the mind upon concealed objects till they expose themselves has so far exposed only the clothes of the soul where men

---

[4] Charcot, Jean-Martin (1825-1893) a French medical researcher who defined the pathology of several nerve and joint diseases and whom Freud studied with to understand something they called *hysteria*.

have looked toward the soul itself. And no man is ready yet to say that soul is the final body he is looking for. No one is ready yet to say that it is the Self of himself he is seeking. The Brahmins taught that it was the Self that never grows old or changes, the one that never thinks or desires, the one that never heard of loving, the Being that never heard or spoke of truth, that they were seeking.

One might finally ask what is all the good, or what is any part of the good, of man seeking for the self that never ages or decays. You know that it is the push of every creature to find the best. The best is that which is free and in bliss. The push of creation is the orbit it is traveling. As the stars move on to their points in the heavens, so creation moves on to its bliss.

The operations of nature are the clothing of man's will. The operations of destiny are the clothing of his mind. The experiences of freedom from nature and destiny are the clothing of his soul. And his soul folds him around with its still more profound mystery.

When the will has confidence in itself it finds all nature meek. When mind has confidence in itself, it finds destiny meek. When soul has confidence in itself, it is free from nature and destiny. It has no use for nature's obedience any more than Socrates may have for your rings or gold buttons. The meekness of nature and destiny is not an interesting topic of the Soul.

Understanding that — Soul, Mind, Spirit, Will, are all names used by metaphysicians to express their estimate of the being whose presence we call the Self.

When one calls God by the name Soul, he is full of loving kindness and warmth. To that one, God is life. When a metaphysician speaks of God as Spirit, he is free and unburdened. To him, God is freedom from the clothing we call flesh. When one calls God, Mind or Intelligence, he is clothed with knowledge. We are astonished at his right knowledge. His memory, his understanding, his judgment, spring forth through every movement, word, look. When one calls God, Substance, there is a substantial quality about his character, his possessions, his words. When one calls God, Omnipresence, he is fitting himself to diffuse and spread himself through the Universe. When one calls God, Omnipotence, he feels his own powerfulness. When one calls God, Omniscience, he shows forth a great wisdom.

The wonderfulness of describing God is that man becomes visibly what he has described- A confidence in himself as actually being 'all that he describes, comes to him. This confidence is called faith. The brother of Jesus Christ called faith a healing quality of mind. "Faith shall save the sick." [James 5:15]

In simple Science, Mind, Will, Soul, Spirit are one God, and thus all confidence of the will is called confidence of God, all confidence of mind, soul, is confidence of God.

With this simple Science continually in mind for a starting point, a working efficiency of mind is recognized. It is great joy to mind to discover that it compels nature, destiny, body and action of every kind by its own thoughts. For the practical purposes of life we might deal only with mind and its thoughts and by simple contemplation compel everything to obey our decrees. As Eliphaz, quoting from the law well known to mystics, says: "Thou shalt decree a thing and it shall be established unto thee." [Job 22:28]

But in dealing steadily with mind, we arrive at sight of another intelligence superior to mind. We grant that superior intelligence the entire right of way. We gladly call the mind which we used in making decrees a non-est ["not existing" or "not-being," nonexistent, nothing] claim. The writers of the books of both the Old and New Testaments are all for the most part dealing with this mind of ours which has the ability to handle material things without appearing to touch them,

When you pray for your friend to be cured, you are using your mind. At a certain point of experience in praying, you have confidence that your friend will be cured. This confidence is a living, bracing tonic in the atmosphere. He receives it and revives. If we then undertake to explain the state of mind that cures the sick, we declare that it is faith. But if the friend were looked upon in the first place as never sick, then we would not have had to rise up faith. Our faith by which we declare we cured our friend may be found at last to be only our mind opening itself to see our friend in his right state.

What is his right state? His state of reality. Have you never heard of people, agonizing in prayer till they saw that it was useless to go any further, for they saw that their friend would never get well this side of the grave? Do you think they saw the reality of that friend's life? Was it not rather that they saw the limit of their own mind and did not spring beyond it? We have now agreed as a Christian people that the Jesus Christ power in man is his power to raise the dead. Jesus found that the prayer of the righteous man would prevail over disease and misfortune. But disease and misfortune are not there to prevail over. What is it that makes disease and misfortune? It is mind. Mind has a substance within itself out of which it forms its body which it calls flesh. Mind has a power to annul its own formulations with which it has clothed itself. All the mind needs to do to unformulate its clothing, is to rouse its confidence.

Spiritual Science means looking at mind's native possibilities and at mind's abilities. It also means looking to see what mind is.

When a man is sick, his mind causes the sickness. When you saw him sick, your mind saw his mind's opinion. If you rally your confidence to strike off the chains of his sickness, you are only engaging in a mental, fight with him. That one of you who is strongest will win.

But who is That standing back of you both that never sees chains? Does That Being know anything at all? Does the mind that is capable of talking about sickness, resemble the Intelligence that never knows sickness?

So the divisions of mind into mortal and immortal have been made. The mortal mind sees and talks of sickness through its instruments, the tongue and eyes. It formulates all deformities, all ugliness. It sometimes
formulates beautiful objects. But it is never the central fire. It is never the Mind that formulates nothing, which like an unnamed, undescribed splendor stands back of mortal mind and shines through its chains. Simple Science calls this intelligence which does no manufacturing of human conditions, by the terms "Immortal Mind," "Immortal Will," "Immortal Spirit," "Immortal God."

It is called true faith when mortal mind does not do anything. Mortal mind parts itself. The less it knows, the less it speaks, the less it acts, the more visible does immortal mind seem to us.

All treatments in mental healing are the struggles of mortal mind to be absent. All faith is the confidence of mortal mind in itself or in what is real, but out of sight. That which manufactures prosperity is mortal mind. For I say unto you that the immortal mind knows neither poverty nor riches, though it knows that these words are a winding sheet of ugliness or beauty to mortal mind. That which causes prosperity is called God. But the God that causes prosperity is mortal mind speaking of the true God who would not be immaculate if He caused prosperity.

The immaculate God knows no opposites.

When mortal mind stretches itself to win a cure of poverty and feels that it will never win the cure, we may see that its confidence in the God that is looking through it is wholly oblivious of the poverty, is not roused at all.

The whole aim of metaphysics so far as faith and works are in any way concerned, is to rouse confidence to the pitch of breaking open mortal mind for Immortal Mind to gleam through. The new charms of life are exposed. Even the formulations of mortal mind catch new beauties.

The Chinese sage whom they revere, is the one who kept himself always at the age of sixteen years by never letting his mortal mind speak. He taught that the wise man, instead of aiming to acquire knowledge should avoid knowledge. Not to act is the source of all power. He saw how full of formulating power the thoughts of the mortal mind are, while in the immortal mind all is finished and nothing has to be made.

Moses caught sight of this when he said that all things were created perfect and were already, before they appeared upon the earth. The fourth lesson of Spiritual Science shows that Moses was speaking of. The Mind that is not identified with flesh and blood and is not identified with the mind that forms them.

That which said, "Let there be," was superior to that which obeyed, and that which obeyed was the outer world. Its whole nature is obedience. But it was mortal mind that was used as the tongue and actor. The language that was used shows that it was the movement of mortal mind itself to stand aside for Immortal Mind to shine through.

"Let there be a firm mind," is the command to a shifting, changing, fleeting set of thoughts to part themselves and let another mind be clearly seen. It was the command which we now often make to our own mind to be still that God may be all. Whoever does this, in reality, finds that firm mind, that changeless undeviating God he is seeking. He gets the result of obeying himself. Then all things are well with him. He finds his very body permeated and diffused with that firm mind. It is the all to him. We experience this in a lesser or greater degree and call it faith. In a lesser degree, we may even say that we have confidence that great good is coming to us. In another degree, we are independent of good or ill. That which is entirely independent of good or ill is the true God. When one rises to the intensity of saying, "Thy will be done," instead of holding his own will so violently, he has risen to faith. The curtains of his mortal mind part and fade for the mighty Will of the Immortal Mind to be made visible on his pathway. There is no word for this Will. It has taken the place of the will that speaks.

It is the providence of Spiritual Science to make mind know the modus operandi of its own departure that that which is real may be realized. There are not among us any who have yet taught their mind to draw its own curtains aside and cause itself to vanish utterly. The religions of the world have not yet been understood so that the freedom men seek has been demonstrated in them. They have found mortal mind entrenched as a determined

Master. But mortal mind is nothing. It is unreality. It seems to itself to be something strong and mighty, but is entirely unseen by the divine fire of intelligence that is the true God in and through all.

It is the mortal mind men have been calling God; but it never was God and never can be God. He who watches this truth is promised the absolute freedom from human experiences which religion is expected to bring. It is not our construction but our quickening and illumination which we are taught by our own soul life to expect by mental changes. Religion shows mental changes.

"We shall not all die; but we shall all be changed," [1 Corinthians 15:51] said Paul. But Paul had to step on into the next sphere without this demonstration of religious freedom.

"Be ye transformed by the renewing of your mind." [Romans 12:2] This transformation we call faith. It is clear sight of the firm mind of the one indestructible God.

There are the remnants of ten great religious systems on the earth, all having their descriptions of God nearly identical. They describe the unchangeable, firm, eternal Mind which our mortal mind falters at the sight of. In addition to Christianity, they are:

1. Egyptian worship;
2. the Hindu faiths of India, which are Brahaminism polished, refined and irresistible; and
3. Buddhism, a later form of Brahaminism more given to demonstrations of healing, raising the dead, hypnotic exercise and feats of formulating and unformulating matter;
4. the Hebrew religion;

5. the Arabian religion, which is [Islam, the followers of] Mohammed;
6. the two Chinese religions, Taoism, and
7. the doctrine of Confucius;
8. the religion of Persia, Zoroastrianism [or Parsi]; and
9. the philosophical systems of Socrates, Plato and Aristotle.

They all describe the mortal mind, which is the semblance and claim of intelligence without origin and without substance. They tell us that we must stand aside in the battle of life and let the warrior within us fight all our battles. This "WE" that is to stand aside, they call the ego, sometimes the lord of life, and sometimes carnal man. Our Scriptures call it carnal man. The early Spiritual Scientists call it mortal mind. Often when men speak of God, they mean the ego of man or the lord of his life, that which rules him. Thus they describe a changeable, arbitrary task master. To describe and look toward such a being is to forget how to rouse the mind to part itself for the firmament to be exposed.

Thus, Jesus Christ asked, "When the Son of man cometh shall He find faith on the earth?" [Luke 18:8]

The prevalent description of mortal mind with its unreliable kindness and its perverse cruelties has caused mind to stop far short of opening its two-leaved gate for the firm Mind of the changeless God, whose Name is beyond God, to have all things in His keeping.

The affirmations of Spiritual Science quicken and hasten mind toward giving up all that it claims to see, for that which it does not see to have the field. Paul said, "Faith is the substance of things hoped for, the evidence of things not seen." [Hebrews 11:1]

All these religions, which are now found to have been the background of Spiritual Science, described faith as that firm-quality of mind which stands and sees what to all sensation and to all appearances from history and circumstances is impossible. It is the fruit which throws the husks aside. The higher our affirmations, the more faith we have, for the wider open mortal mind divides itself like the husks of the berry.

"Let there be a firm mind in the midst of the waters." [Genesis 1:6]

The Hindus practicing Buddhism strive by lofty feelings to burst the bounds and escape from themselves. They call all mind, all will, all destiny and human conditions, "clothing," "robes," "bounds," "bands." They seek freedom from these things which fold them so closely that they seem to be themselves.

The Mohammedans [more accurately, Muslims] practice denying god, by which they mean mortal mind, and affirming God, by which they mean Immortal Mind, saying, "There is no god but God."

The Brahmins deny God that they may affirm God. "From the highest state of Brahma to the lowest straw, all is delusion."

There is one Substance that stands as the body of all the robes of delusion. That is the firmament of the universe. In the metaphysics of Aristotle, this is called Energy.

The highest affirmations we can make express the most energy. They make it impossible for mortal mind to even claim to exist. In the midst of the waters of thoughts stands the unalterable One. We become nothing, for that One to be All. This is our farthest spring of thought. It exposes the One.

I am free from God that God may be God.

LESSON V

There are but twelve statements in religious science. All Bibles give the twelve. There are multitudes of ways of expressing these twelve statements. The power of the whole twelve may be in one statement. Then a Christian like Peter may convert three thousand men by one sermon. A statement of Truth is an axiom. Suppose a man says, "I am the way, the truth, and the life," he is making a statement. He may tell you that he does not believe in statements, but he is giving you one when he repeats this affirmation of Jesus Christ.

The interior life is the Jesus Christ life. Whoever shows you how to get acquainted with the Jesus Christ of you, of the ego of you merged in the divine light of the Absolute, is giving you one or two or three statements of Spiritual Science doctrine and may be indeed giving you the whole twelve.

It is excellent to be orderly in housework, it is excellent to be orderly in temple work. The mind is the temple of the ego. The ego is the "I" that thinks and talks. The "I" that thinks and talks becomes the Absolute when it talks with the Absolute. It becomes the Absolute when it thinks of the Absolute. It dissolves, for the Absolute to be all in all. The light of such thinking and talking falls down straight into sight of all men, Stephen talked of heaven and of angels till even the men who were stoning him saw his face as it had been the face of an angel. It is possible to have the thoughts and speech of the mind so orderly that nothing disorderly can stay therein any more than in an orderly home.

The First Chapter of Genesis gives this order. So does the Book of Revelation by St. John.

1. The premise, There is only God. "The Word".
2. The denial of the reality of all but God.
3. The affirmation of all as Good or as God. "Salvation".
4. The faith of mind in God as Truth. "Faith"
5. The work of mind having faith in God. "Works"
6. The understanding which illuminates mind when talking and thinking of God. "Wisdom"
7. The healing of all things of belief in any other birth but the Spiritual. It is the denial of the reality of lustful passions and sensual appetites. There is no origin of creation except in Spirit. "Generation"
8. The denial of appearances of other substance end character than Spirit. The disallowance of psychology, suggestion, hypnotism, magnetic or mesmeric influences. There is but one influence, one informer, and that is God.' There is no deception. "Light"
9. The disannulment of sin. The rejection of the idea of sin. As God is all, there can be no sin. "Holiness"
10. The true creation must be manifest. It discusses the exposure of health through the chemicalization of seeming disease when truth is told to mind. "Jerusalem"
11. The disallowment of foolishness and ignorance. They are not present, The Bible denies them. "Judgment"
12. All is the perfect creation of the living God manifest everywhere "Praise"

These twelve propositions or aphorisms of Science were all given by Jesus in His own language. They read this way:
1. God is Spirit and they that worship Him must worship Him in Spirit.
2. Ye are of your father the devil, a lie from the beginning. One is your Father, even God. Judge not according to appearance.
3. The Father and I are One. I in you.
4. Ye believe in God, believe also in Me.
5. These signs shall follow them that believe,
6. I will give you a mouth and wisdom which all your adversaries shall not be able to gainsay nor resist. God giveth not the Spirit by measure.
7. Call no man upon earth your father.
8. Ye are the light of the world.
9. I came not to condemn the world.
10. Heaven and earth shall pass away, but My Word shall not pass away.
11. Ye all know from whence I am. The Holy Ghost shall teach you all things.
12. All things that I have heard from the Father I have told you. Your joy no man taketh from you.

Many other passages go with each of these. Peter said in his first book, second chapter, fourth verse, that this doctrine that all is God is the living stone disallowed of men but chosen of God. Take it and hold the letter or proper reasoning thereof and see how the glory of God will take its seat in your system down to the foundations of your very body.

Did not Paul catch a sight of the entrance of the glorious body of Christ into his own body?

This is the esoteric philosophy or deep Spiritual Science: you have the deep glory of the interior life going on within you. So have all creatures. Science exposes it and keeps it exposed.

The twelve statements of the Bibles of the world have twelve inner glories. They are the 24 elders who fall down out of sight when God is exposed in His glory all over this earth.

When you or any one of you exposes the glory you had with the Father before the world, then there is nothing left on this planet that is dark or speaks of darkness.

The world will not rest a second in its present appearance when one of us appears plainly here as God, interiorly or hiddenly, as we are now God. Exposed or manifest we must be God. This is done by keeping the words of the letter of Spiritual philosophy till the Spirit claims its own.

The gate keeping each of us from this instant speaking aloud and boldly stepping forth as God in our glory, is one statement of criticism. Each prophet hid himself behind a gate of condemnation. Each priest hid himself behind a gate of caste. Each layman hid himself behind a gate of agreement with some prophet or priest. All Bibles make it clear what the gates were which hid their prophets and kings.

The deep Spiritual significance of the twelve propositions of Spiritual Science takes our attention so entirely that these gates are surely burned down. Who shall prevent our glorious God from working when we throw the searchlight of our own independent Sunshine over the universe?

The profound meditation of the Hindus for countless years has now brought us face to face with their gates of hiding and their agreement with our prophets, priests and sages. We show them plainly our gates of hiding. They show us theirs. We show them the light of our gospel of Christ. They show us the light of their gospel of Christ. They are one light. They have the same Truth we have. There is but one Truth. Their criticisms, castes, condemnations are many. Our criticisms, castes, condemnations are legion. They are delusions. They are nothing, and as Daniel explains, "less than nought," but they seem to hide God. They are the "works of the devil," said Jesus. But the devil is a liar and the father of the liar. So a lie is the whole sum and substance of all that hides God.

The Hindus have their sages who express twelve thoughts that shall heal the world. In their philosophy, as explained by the Theosophists, we have these lessons taken from a little book of *Raja Yoga* in the English language, translated from the Sanskrit, as follows

1. Brahman is the all-pervading One.
2. The whole world is Atman and nothing but Atman. Atman is the Omnipresent principle.
3. Sitting in a solitary place being desireless, curbing passions, one should meditate upon the identification of one's self with that Atman who is One and has no distinction of place, things and time. I am that very Brahman.
4. As the identity and unification of one's self and Atman is known, the belief that himself is body, senses, etc., will vanish and one will see in himself that undivided and indivisible Atman.
5. The meaning of Brahman is the Ever-Create. A man becomes that on which he persistently thinks.
6. All this universe, visible and invisible, the seer, the seen, the sight, is one eternal conscious-

ness. The enlightened, through his mind, will be ever filled with the bliss of identifying himself with universal consciousness.

7. He who is free from the great bondage of desires, so difficult to avoid, is alone capable of liberation, not another, though versed in the six systems of philosophy.

8. Disease is never cured by pronouncing the name of medicine without taking it; so liberation is not achieved by the pronunciation of the word Brahman without direct perception. The Spirit must be sought out by intuition. Unmanifested Spiritual consciousness begins to manifest like the dawn in the pure heart and, shining like the mid-day sun, illuminates the whole universe — pure consciousness.

9. Deprived of the real knowledge of the Atman through being devoured by the shark of great delusions, the man becomes contemptible in conduct. The properties of pure *sattva* are purity, perception of the Atman within us, cheerfulness, concentration of mind on the self by which a taste of eternal bliss is obtained.

10. A wise man must acquire discrimination of Spirit and not Spirit in all things, as only by realizing the self in all, which is absolute Being, he becomes bliss.

11. Ignorance has no beginning, and this also applies to its effects; but upon the production of knowledge, ignorance, although without beginning, is entirely destroyed. The knowledge that Brahman and Atman are one and the same is true knowledge. This can only be acquired by the perfect discrimination of ego and non-ego. Ego is the "I" that ordains and knows. The non-ego seems to ordain and know, but is nothing.

12. By the absence of all existence besides itself this Brahman is truth, is supreme, the only One; when the supreme truth is realized fully, nothing remains but this.

All the rest of their lessons revolve around these twelve, as all our Christ doctrines swing around twelve.

The mind of man has its "I" which ordains and moves. This is called the human ego. The Supreme God who knows only Himself, is the substance upon which the human ego relies for its movements as our shadows rely upon us for their movements. We know that our shadows have no life or substance, so the Supreme God knows that the ego of human-kind has no life or substance, and that its blessedness is its being lost in the Supreme.

Is it not the highest good of my shadow to be lost in me? Is it not the highest good of me to be God? Thus shall earthly shadows flee. Thus shall human egotisms vanish at the turn of their language toward the Absolute.

All men in supreme moments have seen that there was nothing to" worship, but there was something to be. John tried to adore the angel, but the angel told him once for all he was not greater than John. Both were turning their speech and thought toward the divine truth of life in such a fashion that soon they would be dead as flesh and celestial and alive as God.

When we hear this truth, it is our business to speak forth to the schools, the churches, the business mind of the race. No matter what they say or do with us, we shall not die as majesty and strength, for majesty and strength are the unkillable breath of the Supreme Presence.

Truth was in the uncounted past and whoever told it was majestic and strong. Truth is in the living present and whoever tells it is majestic and strong. Truth will be the same in the future and whoever tells it will be majestic and strong.

Joseph had been brought up under the shadow language of talk about his youth, his limitations, his inferiority. He rose up boldly and told the sons of Bilhah and Xilpah that he was king and lord over their opinions. He told the schools and churches of the globe that his Supreme God has asserted Itself and that no man, no climate, no school, no church, could be greater than His greatness. So he mastered by what seemed to be the stroke of chance, but which was the natural working forth of Truth.

The Supreme Truth is that which is always supreme. Nothing can defeat it. Nothing can kill it. Its ministry is to invest me with strength, beauty and immortality like itself. It is the stream of eternal youth, of immortal beauty, of unchanging majesty. Those who knew Truth were said in the past to stay always as 16 years of age in looks. The story of Joseph is to show that 17 years is the look of that face and figure which asserts that it is master of life and death and the commandments of men, and which knows that it is in its essence God, the Supreme.

What shall be the look of that one who perceives that the Truth is the Supreme in the sense of the Only One? What is there for this Truth to reign over? Shall that which is alone in its splendor reign over what to it has no presence? What does the Truth know of what is not Truth?

What is the body formed of Truth alone? Whose face of thought, speech, action, is turned to Truth alone? How does he look? He is in our midst.

LESSON VI

Paracelsus[5] told his neighbors that if they wished to awaken their inherent magical powers, they should continually read the book of Revelation by St. John. Magical powers are the esoteric or hidden faculties which all men possess. Confucius[6] said that if any man would stimulate these faculties he would not need to study books. There would be an understanding of the substance contained in the books akin and superior to the mind which wrote them.

The book of St. John is a statement of a great mind directed toward our magical powers. There is a practice of directing mind toward bodily conditions and bringing out their health and beauty. This was the first claim to attention made by Mrs. Eddy's book, *Science and Health*. There is a practice of directing special attention toward the eyes of vision and causing them to see plainly; there is a practice of attending strictly to the eyes of mental understanding and drawing aside the ideas that obscure wisdom. These lessons are intended to accomplish this result. There is one for drawing out the magical powers. The book of Revelation works this miracle. It takes about an hour to read it; which was the

---

[5] Paracelsus, Philippus Aureolus [1493-1541] (aka Theophrastus Bombastus von Hohenheim): Swiss-born alchemist and physician whose books were standard medical texts for centuries.
[6] Confucius [K'ung Fu-tzu] - Chinese philosopher [551-479 B.C.]; Author of the Analects, one of the six Chinese classics carved upon stone between 175-183 A.D., a compilation of exhortations to high moral living.

length of time devoted by Mrs. Eddy's students to one treatment of a case that did not promptly respond. The book of Revelation is in figurative language and refers to the breaking forth of the great judgment and understanding in one mind, in all minds everywhere. Then all the powers of mind are found ours. We use them skillfully.

St. John continually addresses the inner ears of the mystic body as, "He that hath ears to hear, let him hear what the Spirit saith." Luke, the physician, in his gospel continually addresses the chord in us which is the love of God. We have one, whoever we may be, and being treated, it awakes. He calls it "Theophilus." Commentators on Luke have wondered who "Theophilus" could be. His name, meaning "love of God," tells the story.

When Mrs. Eddy wrote *Science and Health*, she brought out the principle of treatment the best it had ever been discussed. Whenever we commune with anybody or anything in any way or fashion, we treat them. We may not mean to do so, or we may mean to do so, the result is the same. The more you understand of a subject, the clearer your comrades will be on that subject. Your knowledge is a "treatment."

Aristides[7] told Socrates that his wisdom penetrated him whenever he approached him and he felt more like the wisdom of Socrates, "Therefore, get wisdom, and with thy getting, get understanding." "They that have understanding among the people shall be wise and do exploits."

There is one Presence that we cannot elude or get absent from. It is the presence of Supreme Wisdom. It is God. If we look towards this presence con-

---

[7] Aristides [530? - ?468 B.C.], "the Just:" Athenian statesman during Socrates' lifetime.

tinually, we look like it. We are always images of what we are looking at. The mind looks at the presence of Wisdom and shines till every part and particle of the body is transfigured. It is by the human mind or mortal mind thinking about the Divine Immortal Mind that the Divine Immortal Mind shines upon it and through it. Finally, the shine of the Immortal Mind on the mortal mind discloses the tremendous fact that there is no reality or substance or presence or claim or anything whatsoever of the mortal or human.

When a speaker is telling about mind as an instrument, he is quoting from the doctrine of the Brahmins on the mortal or the human mind. He does not mean the Great Presence whose name is Immortal, Divine Understanding. That is not an instrument. It does not speak our language, yet when we look toward it we speak a language. It does not think anything, yet when we look toward it we think thoughts. We hear speakers and we read writers and they say, "There is one Mind thinking thoughts. It is the only Mind. It is Divine, Immortal Wisdom." They mean this great Presence whose influence is so powerful upon our mind when we look toward it that we think like new creatures.

Then again speakers and writers use the term "Ego" for both the human one in you which governs the body and the "Divine Ego" who knows nothing of the body.

You must have what the Theosophists call "discriminative knowledge" and separate promptly and without error the ego human from the Ego Divine. You must separate promptly and without error, the human or mortal mind from the Divine Immortal Mind. You must separate physically visible material nature from spiritually visible Spirit. Some speakers and writers talk more of nature and intellect. Examine them closely and you perceive they are describing the unreal delusive phenomena of the physically visible world of matter. It is an interesting system, but it is not Spirit. It is what Mrs. Eddy calls the dream creation. It is what the Buddhists call *maya*, or delusion.

If the speaker or writer tells you that it is of delusion he is speaking, you feel the knowledge of truth spring up at once. It is a good treatment of the chord in your being, which is "the separator," as our Bible terms it; "the discriminator," as the Eastern books term it. It is the final dissolving of outside nature to know it as delusion and unreality. It is the exposure of reality and glory.

Suppose you think the substance of the quinine pill is God? It will act like a drawing to one side of curtains on the quinine pills. The power of God will stand out from it. It will have a healing effect. God is health whenever spoken of in any way or anywhere. Suppose you say that the substance of your voice, the substance of your glance of eye, the substance of your touch, is God? The power of God will be exposed by so saying. Everything you do will have a healing quality.

The very mention of God is the mention of a healing power. One name of God is Christ Jesus. It is a wonderful discloser of covered faculties to look toward the Christ Jesus in all things. The greatest miracles are wrought by looking toward the Name of the Great Presence of Wisdom.

No matter what errors you keep in your mind, you can be a miracle worker, if you look toward this mighty presence whose most miraculous Name is Christ Jesus. You may even believe that there is a devil, like Gasner,[8] who cured all kinds of disease by

---

[8] Really Johann Joseph Gassner (1727- 1779, in what is now Bavaria)

applying the name Jesus Christ to the men and women as a present irresistible health. You may call God a great Person sitting on a throne as the faith-cure workers of our own time do, who do indeed cure all manner of disease by applying the name Christ or Christ Jesus to the people as a present irresistible health.

Errors count nothing — simply nothing — while you are looking so steadily toward this almighty Presence here just before us.

The way we have of looking toward this Presence best is by talking to it. Hosea said, "Let us take with us words and go unto our God." Mary, the Mother of Jesus, did not speak. Her mind was not thinking a single thought. This gave the Wisdom now looking at us, the free passage through her mind. We are able to be as free to the transit of an unprejudiced idea through us by keeping our mind facing the divine Mind till the divine is all there is of us.

There is an instant after speaking when we do not speak. There is an instant after thinking when we do not think. This instant is the silence in heaven which Mary felt. She brought forth a Wonderful Counselor, a Mighty God, by being entirely divine. We may bring forth our own ordained works by being so lost in the sight of this Presence that we are It only.

The Arabians taught of the drawing power, the irresistibility of it, by the story of the mountain which, when a ship should sail in sight of it, would cause the craft to go all to pieces. The nails, the steel bands, the iron chains, the metal fastenings and tools would leave the ship and fly to the mountain. The wood, hay and stubble of the ship would

---

gained a wide celebrity by professing to "cast out devils" and to work cures on the sick by means simply of prayer.

disappear. So we, if we sail the ship of our mind toward the mountain of God, here in our midst, by thinking and thinking of God, shall be no more human beings, but transcendent, divine beings. We shall be what the genuine quality, the true substance of us, already is — God manifest. The mind, which we have called an instrument, will be wood, hay, stubble. It will be pure nothingness. The Christ Jesus mind will be all there is of us.

The flesh as a changing, homely, hateful, even as a loveable thing, will be gone. The mind, with its errors, with its strife to be true, will be gone. Only the eternal body in its beauty, only the Divine Mind with its brilliant understanding will be left. "For we know that if our earthly house of this tabernacle were dissolved, we have a building of God, an eternal habitation."

This is what all science, all religion, all books, all philosophy, every study, are trying to expose. Understanding is the well-spring of life.

In Mrs. Eddy's book, which first introduced Christian Science as a healing principle, we find the idea that Understanding is the divine Self at work. That is, if one sits in the presence of a sick person and understands that his disease is delusion — nothing, and understands that really he is divinely whole and perfect, the patient is sure to get well at once. His divine spiritual nature comes forward and he shows good health. On this same principle, an idiotic child has a brilliant mind at the center of his being, and if any of us understand this to be true, the intelligence of that child will come forward in proportion to our understanding. David said that by understanding the heavens are formed and the earth and all things therein. Understanding is One. It is all in all as the sun is all in all of the atmosphere. Focused on the idiotic child's gross appearance, it burns it off as the focus of the sun's rays upon any object burns it off.

We learn a habit of concentrating our own understanding upon one thing or another according to what science we are studying. If we are studying the Yoga books, we shall call understanding by the term "discriminative knowledge." We shall be told upon what to focus our attentive mind—almost always upon some material thing. Then we will find the ego, or central intelligence of that thing and it will expose certain wonderful information. For instance, we are told to concentrate our mind upon the moon and directly we will know all about the fixed stars. But pure Spiritual Science recommends fixing the mind upon the God here present. Jesus Christ said, "Seek first the kingdom of God, and all these things will be added unto you."

It is my business to distinguish and distinguish instantly, between the concentration of mind on one universal Spirit equally present everywhere and the concentration of mind on the nose or on the moon or even on a word. The Buddhists and Brahmins teach that to concentrate the mind upon such a word as "friendship" will draw friends to us as to magnets.

Jesus is the friend unto whom the world now turns, and His whole attention was fixed on the one God here present, whom to understand is to be exactly like, the same in all qualities, the same in all powers.

Though one teacher may be telling of the soul that sinneth, and another may tell that the soul is sinless God, shall you be distracted? Though one may talk of a wounded spirit, and another may tell of the spirit that is free from all that transpires, free to be a spectator of the great delusion of the universe or not see it, the one Free Spirit, who is the untouchable God, shall you be distracted? Though one may tell of the mind that makes mistakes today and does wisely tomorrow, while another man shall say that Mind never makes mistakes, for it is God, shall you be distracted? Though one teacher may talk of mind as if there were two minds, viz., a human mind and a divine mind, shall you think there are two minds? Would you say there were two boats because you saw a reflection of your boat in the water under you? Is there any human spirit in reality? Is there any mortal or deluded mind in reality? Is there any human or carnal man in reality? If I speak of one, can you tell instantly whether I speak of the unreal boat that glides under our real boat or of the boat we are sailing in? If I speak of the mind as an instrument, do you know instantly whether I am speaking of what glides along dealing with things material or of that One Intelligence from whose storehouse we draw understanding of how to handle the mind we use? If I speak of man, are you instantly cognizant of whether I am speaking of God, or of an inverted image of God?

Do you know why we speak the most unbelievable and wonderful things to a world which has all its attention turned toward matter? It is because mind pulls the material things around with it. Shall you not love to seethe prophecies of the good and noble of all ages fulfilled, when, by our understanding, we have straightened up all downcast and beautified all imperfect things? This is promised to be the first signal of the understanding firewithin us being focused on God, whose name is Understanding.

Do you realize that we must speak of understanding if we would understand well? Do you realize that if you want to see the fine fleet of light that streams between the small air globules that close around us, you must watch for it and think about it constantly?

Do you realize that there is one topic upon which you can fix your human mind that will erase the human mind and show the Divine Mind? Do you know what you ought to fix your grieved soul upon till your soul that is capable of grieving is lost and the soul that is above all human passions is present?

"Come and let us reason together." Let us attend to our own sunshine, our own God nature. Shall not we be the God that sets the unhappy world into peace? Shall we not be the hot fire that shall consume the dross that now covers the brightness of men and women and children?

It is by understanding our own splendor that we burn down the barriers that hide our ears from hearing the wonderful choirs that are now singing near us. It is by understanding our own hot splendor of Intelligence that we burn off the scales that hide the sight of what is going on around us.

There comes a moment when understanding springs forth in some direction.

One man's understanding heals all manner of disease wheresoever he walks. One man lets a streak of bright sunshine go free by much thought on the way of the Spirit, and wherever he walks he speaks brilliantly, originally, powerfully of God. We wonder at him. One man lets his sunshine of understanding stream through him toward the world by focusing his thoughts till they burn through unhappiness. Everybody is happy when his mind thinks of them.

Thinking of God, we are thinking of a fire that will consume everything except itself; therefore, as our walls feel the flames, we are all illuminated, inspired, on some line. We work miracles on that line. Thinking and still thinking of God, we feel the fires of His burning taking down other gates and we work other miracles. Thinking and thinking of God, we burn down still other bars, still more plastering; we work other miracles. Thinking and thinking of God we find ourselves God. We do all things. The former heaven and earth are no longer visible to us. We are the light of our world as God is the light. We are the heat of our world -as God is the heat of the universe. Thinking and thinking of God melts the rocks and the mountains. Thinking and thinking of God dissolves flesh, the glorious body of Jesus Christ which was with us before the world was, which is with us now, and which we never can get away from, is visible. We are not changing, discordant creatures. We, by thinking of God, understand God. We do not have to walk among sorrowful beings. Thinking and thinking of God, we understand the God who speaks as man or as beast everywhere.

How much God intelligence has shed Itself through you now? Do you see upright, irresistible men and women and horses? Are they out of the reach of pain or hunger in your eyes? Does everyone look handsome, healthy, brilliant with wisdom, in your eyes?

How long have you been making God the one theme upon which you have fed your mind? Do you eat the Name of God with your mind as you eat your breakfast? Do you eat the Name Jesus Christ with your mind as you eat your dinner? Is God all in all to you? Through and through you? Do you understand why the Name Jesus Christ is a Name that burns and cracks the plastered walls that have kept you appearing in a house of flesh and blood, skin and bone? Is it because that Name stands for one that took the human mode of thoughts and fed them on God till the understanding of God made that mind all God? It is because that Name stands for one mind that took a human appearance and ate the Name God; that loved the One Presence, that concentrated upon the one Spirit till the glorious spiritual body shone out in full sight. It is because that Name stands for one who, though drawn into the appearance, kept calling Himself God and would not be other than God for one instant. He would not forget His own Substance. He conquered by conscious knowledge of His Spiritual origin and everlasting quality. He made the earth a plaything. He handled its serpents as one that knows himself the master of serpents, through conscious acquaintance with God. He called health into sight, life into sight, through making health and life as obedient as serpents, by conscious knowledge of God, whose presence will fire you with understanding of how to handle life, health, strength, peace.

Jesus Christ is a Name that stands for one who dwells at the center and moves Life and Spirit through the Universe, or does nothing with life and Spirit, according to choice. When we turn our mind toward that Name, we are arriving at the same freedom. All men have the Jesus Christ freedom at their center. When I understand Jesus Christ through thinking of God as Jesus Christ, through meditating upon the Name as the Brahmins meditate upon One, I shall be Jesus Christ in the new Name which no human tongue speaks, which no man knows who sees anything whatsoever that hurts or discourages.

Whoever understands God through concentrating upon the Name Jesus Christ has the Holy Ghost power. Whoever understands God through concentrating all the attention of his mind upon the Name, Jesus Christ, remembers all that he knew with God in the beginning and can tell boldly and brilliantly all that he now knows. Concentrating the sun rays, we burn the wood, hay, stubble. Concentrating all the God seen into the Name Jesus Christ, we burn away sorrow and foolishness, matter and mind.

To understand is to believe or not believe wisely. If we understand God through concentration of mind upon the Name Jesus Christ, we do not believe in the reality of matter, we do not believe that evil or sickness can conquer. We believe that the Spirit of man will rise in unconquerable majesty if we see it in a man. We believe the Spirit will rise in him and be noble, healthy, beautiful. We see it in all men present; therefore, we believe in it and testify that we do see. And our testimony is true.

The divine Pemender[9] saith, "These things, O Asclepius, will appear to be true if you understand them; but if thou understandest them not, incredible. For to understand is to believe; but not to believe is not to understand."

We understand God through feeding the mind on a Name. The Name rushes from center to circumference of all things now. We hold no longer on to the Name. We are the Name. We eat no more of God. We are God. We speak no longer of Jesus Christ. We are Jesus Christ. We are not human. We are divine. We are not seeking to understand. We are understanding. We are not in the world or of the world. We are all that is.

"Is there anything besides me? Nay, I know not anything." To know myself is understanding. I understand myself; therefore, I understand all there is to understand. I am all; therefore, all understand. Hath it not been written that the understanding of one is the understanding of all?

---

[9] Asclepius is the Greek god of healing, known in Latin as Aesculapius. Pemender is not historical, but may be a character in one of the Greek plays that Emma was familiar with.

LESSON VII

After the mind is dissolved from the claim of being an instrument into the knowledge of being God, the whole world, with all its people, the whole canopy of heaven with all its stars, all things above, beneath and around, are exposed to their actuality.

It is the Adam mind that sees God and names Him animal, plant, bird, human nature. The Christ Mind sees God and has a language of his vision which the Adam mind comprehends not. Everything has a language of its own in imitation of the language of the Absolute. The wrens that chatter in the trees understand their own language. The heart beats while the head is cool and indifferent. Something addresses the heart which the eyes cannot see, as something addresses the ears which the hands cannot touch. And each of these conversations is the signal to us of the one speech of God going on all the time. Only God understands God. It is the highest speech that tongue can offer concerning the ears and their language to say that they do not hear. This leaves God alone as hearing. It is the highest speech that the. tongue can tell of the language of the eyes to say that they do not see. God is the only sight. It is the highest speech the tongue can utter concerning the language of the mind to say that it does not think. This leaves the only Mind to be the Mind that is God.

"Be still and know that I am God," is the language of that Mind of which mind is the symbol. Only the language of the Absolute is a true language. It is only from knowledge of the Absolute that we can be wise.

The stillness which is enjoined upon what are called our organs of sense or our faculties, with all their peculiar tongues, is making them all plastic receptacles for the inpouring of the Absolute. Perfect stillness is entire openness. Entire openness is the reception of the All-Knowledge.

On small and imitative scales, we see this principle operated by the photographic plate which takes the contour of a large object, and also by a man's mind which becomes negative for you to imprint your whole character upon him so that he is called a character reader. For him to be entirely plastic to you would be his being lost into your being and will. Thus we have the still possibility of being entirely lost in the Absolute -- which is our reasonable service, as Paul declared.

"Not my will, but Thine, be done," said Jesus.

You can see that no man would be so powerful as he who had resolved himself unto God. This is meekness, which is Omnipotence.

"He that is greatest among you, let him be your servant," said Jesus Christ. "1 am meek and lowly of heart." "I have overcome, the world." "All power is given unto Me in heaven and in earth."

Seventhly, then, in scientific order of concentration of the Absolute, Moses said the earth should bring forth works. "Let the earth bring forth." So mind, made nothing as an instrument, becomes by such meekness, brilliant with understanding and serves like Jesus Christ. It brings forth. Water is meek to its thought or to its spoken word. It changes into wine. It will change into whatever substance you please.

The body of mankind is meek as water to one who has himself risen from entire openness to entire wisdom. Nobody can withstand your orders. You are Jesus Christ in fact. To Jesus Christ every knee shall bow. The Jesus Christ Mind is wide awake — widely open consciousness. It does no miracles accidentally. It is as thoroughly competent to do the next miracle that is presented as the first one. Why do not Christians work every miracle with prompt and equal skill? Their miracles are not the work of understanding. They are not conscious of Themselves.

The book of Genesis teaches the consciousness of Mind. To read the first chapter is to find ourselves waking up to our God Mind by loosing our hold of our mortal mind.

Conscious miracle working is consciousness of God. The miracles need not to be wrought in the estimation of one who has no mind, no life, no thought, no language, but lets whatever is, remain as it is. It is the Jesus Christ wisdom that sees God in the tree and sees no tree, sees God in the convict and sees no convict.

When that which is true is mentioned, it is exposed. This is bringing forth.

When that which has no time is mentioned, it is exposed. This is bringing forth. When that which never heard of death or life is mentioned, it is exposed. This is bringing forth. When that which never heard of mind is mentioned, it is exposed. This is bringing forth.

The language of the heart is reported by the tongue. The language of the ears is reported by the tongue. The language of the life is reported by the tongue. The language of death is reported by the tongue. Therefore, Solomon says, "Death and life are in the power of the tongue." And again, he says, "The tongue of the wise is health."

The language of that which thinks not of life or death is reported by the tongue. The language of what is absolutely changeless is reported by the tongue. The curtains of sight are closed when the tongue reports the language of the ears only. While one describes wonderful music perfectly, we do not see the music nor see the reporter. Eyesight is forgotten. The ears are deaf while a wonderful painting or a wonderful face gazes toward us. So all the senses of man, so all the mind and thought of man, are still when the tongue tells skillfully the language of God or that which is and alters not. "Eye hath not seen, nor ear heard, neither hath it entered into the heart of man to conceive what God hath prepared for them that love Him."

The sage of India who showed the German traveler some old manuscript books, told him that the true sage never wrote books, never talked, never made effort to teach. He had barred his mind by silencing all its operations to receive the imprint of the ever present Wisdom and whoever should come into his presence would receive what he knew in like manner or remain ignorant.

What that language is which the One-present Being is imprinting on the God-Being at our center, only the God in us knows.

Whatever is unalterable truth must stand forth. This is bringing forth. The nearer the tongue comes to telling the unalterable Truth, the more perfect the bringing forth of health, life, intelligence.

The tongue speaks the language of Omnipresence and the mind designs to extend itself to greatness thereby. But the electric spark that occupies no room is the Omnipresence of the universe. By some clash, it is exposed, and houses are burned and men destroyed. They show themselves to be at their native estate, of the same substance as the spark at its invisible presence. So that by one visibility of the Mind that is not visible to the human mind or to the eyes of man, the whole human mind with all its friendly senses is burned away to be as the spark of that Absolute that stays here and waits.

"The heavens shall roll away as a scroll. The elements shall melt with fervent heat."

We are told in the *Raja Yoga* philosophy of India, that the earth ego is shrouded by five sheaths which right doctrine will dissolve, and that the man ego is shrouded by five sheaths which the right doctrine will dissolve. The right doctrine is the true statement of what God is, what nature is, what man is, what life is.

In a little book of translated aphorisms by Tookeram Tatya, we read, "A wise man must acquire the discrimination of Spirit and not-Spirit, as only by realizing the Self which is Absolute being, consciousness and bliss, he himself becomes bliss."

The "I" that is conscious of the gross body and is hurt or pleased by what happens to the gross body, is the human ego. So long as that which happens in the gross world is observed and changes, we are human ego, human mind. This "I" is one of the sheaths of the divine Spark. By dissolving the human "I" or ego, the shining Absolute breaks forth and the gross body disappears.

All the points of Jesus Christ doctrine are directed to the dissolving of the sheaths of the Soul Ego, or the Divine Spark, the God Self: First, by the right doctrine of the Soul, mind, nature, and matter; Second, by the right doctrine of Ego, God, invisible, un-nameable One; Third, by ceasing from doctrine altogether.

Never till the tongue is speechless, the mind dissolved, the ego melted, can truth be known — be exposed — be brought forth. Then all doctrine is seen to be not.

Then, the "I," the Ego, the so-called God, is seen to be not. Then Truth Absolute, as our language has it at its best, is seen to be not.

[The Taoists remind us,]That which Is, is not that which can be told.

There is something that is free from all union. That is which Is. That which is unattached, is free. That which is free, is God. Hence he who looks toward freedom by doctrine is looking toward God.

To look toward freedom by doctrine is to use an instrument to view the heavens or the insects of earth. Doctrine treats of omnipresence. This is telescopic information. Doctrine treats of the inconceivably small. This is microscopic information. Each takes the mind from its habitual tracks and shows to the senses new territories.

But no doctrine is truth. All doctrine is but an instrument to distract the mind's native knowledge from Truth. The purpose of Jesus Christ is to set mind free from doctrine, to turn it to see the Absolute, and thus, to be the Absolute.

Science teaches to ignore science. Doctrine leads to dropping doctrine. Talk of God leads to no talk of God.

Spiritual Science leads away from science. Spiritual Science dissolves science. It dissolves itself. Its only mission is finished when we know there is nothing to say, for there is nothing to know. The Truth is unknowable by that which is dissolvable.

Truth is known only to itself.

Only God brings forth God. God is what IS.

LESSON VIII

There are three interpretations given to Scripture writings. These interpretations constitute the three great doctrines of men:

(1) Literal
(2) Mental [or Idea]
(3) God [or Spiritual]

Take the words "bottomless pit" as an example. The literalists see and feel according to common sense that there must be a bottomless hole to contain all the billions of existences that have been inhabitants of the universe and will be dwellers here in the future who have trespassed and erred.

The mentalists, or those who resolve everything into mind declare that there is no bottomless pit except in the desire of the mind. Nothing, they explain, can satisfy the mental desire. Give a man everything he asks for, and he is still a sandy plain ready to suck in something else. Desire is bottomless vacuum.

God, being the only One, those who take the passages of Scripture spiritually are found declaring that the God in man swallows all that has being and all that has existence. The unlimited One is the consuming fire which swallows death and hell, heaven and paradise, being and not being. Is it not written that death and hell are swallowed up in victory? Is it not written that Jesus Christ is the victory that swallows death and hell?

Jesus Christ is a Name of God consuming the universe. "I draw all men unto Me." Is it not the word of Jesus Christ that all things are delivered unto Him of the Father? Who so glorious in peace as he who eats and contains all things and is satisfied? It is the Jesus Christ in man that calls for all things to be consumed in his own body. It is God containing God. This is illumination. This is the shining light. This is smokeless fire. This is the light of the world.

Whatever interpretation of Scripture pleases you best is your illumination such as you have. And your illumination is your doctrine. Doctrine acts as a light to the feet and a lamp shining on the pathway to be one's defense and gloriousness, or his Hades[10] and pain. Send on ahead of yourself your proclamation of what is according to your interpretation and you will find every stone and tree moving itself either out of your way to give you free transit or into your way to hinder you when you arrive at that object your doctrine prepared for you. "My word," saith the Lord, "is a lamp unto your feet." "My word," saith Satan, "is plainly spoken by you when you realize satanic conditions.

"The letter killeth," says a bold text. That is, whoever takes the Scripture as it reads literally, must be material and go out as matter goes out, namely, in death. For we find that the letter preaches a doctrine of death; therefore, that letter being a man's highest light arranges his pathway. It is his lantern. It is the doctrine that transfigures and delights the pathway which interprets Scripture as God. He who takes the lake of fire to be a literal, material Hades must have much heat of life's battle. "In the world, ye shall have tribulation." He who finds the lake of fire a hot remorse of mind for his errors has a double torment, for thus

---

[10] Hades is the Greek term for the under-world realm where they believed souls go after death.

both his mind and his body enter into daily tribulation.

Is it any advantage to think that all the blindness there is, is mental - blindness, since mental states shadow themselves on the etheric walls of creation and make bodily states?

To admit that I cannot hear the voice of the Lord will not only shut my mind to the knowledge of God, but will affect my outer ears. Very likely, I will have a number of deaf people making my pathway more difficult daily; but if I tell them the Lord God is the only deafness there is, since one who contains all things cannot hear outside of himself, I find I myself am that one whom I acknowledge and what is not myself I cannot hear.

Such a doctrine turns me toward myself. It is my own word lighting my own mind. I see thereby that I may make some deaf people if I choose. I see that I may have physical deafness if I please. I perceive that I may have a world of people hearing what pleases them and deaf to what does not please them through the doctrine I hold. I see that they may hear what is not pleasing to them if I hold either the interpretations of matter or mind while I read Scriptures. My doctrine is my lamp which lights my life with splendor or lurid haze.

Only the God-interpretation can illuminate my life with what satisfies me. By this lamp I find every object and every event a subdued instrument for my use without effort on my part. My only effort has been the carrying of my doctrine as a man carries a candle.

Things are subject to doctrine. Minds are subject to doctrine. Things and mind are exposed by doctrine.

Why does a man dig in the gold mines, or work shrewdly with his fellowmen to get their gold? Because it is the nature of the doctrine he believes in to compel his efforts in one of these directions.

Could he have a doctrine that would undo effort? He could. This doctrine of Jesus undoes effort of all minds. In the midst of the world of effort, the man with the doctrine of Jesus lies down and sits still while all things arrange themselves in order to please him. As the Scriptures read, "He maketh me to lie down in green pastures." "Your heavenly Father careth." "Take no thought*" "Thy will now be done."

The doctrine of Jesus is the doctrine of ease. It is the doctrine that exposes things that are already formed, for it is the oldest teaching of mankind that things are already created before they appear. He who has right doctrine has a lamp that exposes what is already made; therefore, the principal thing to obtain is right doctrine.

Doctrines are the light that Moses said "Let there be." Disturb them not. Despise them not. Let each man try his own lamp and see what is already made from the light his own doctrine throws upon it.

One man, by his own lamp, sees provisions in abundance in a city that is starving. By steadily keeping that lamp shining on that city, these abundant provisions do exhibit themselves to all the citizens, and the man with the lamp has not stirred from his chair. His doctrine reads: "Plenty for poverty;" "Beauty for ashes;" "The oil of joy for mourning."

Elisha's lamp exposed the horsemen and chariots against whom no army of men could fight. Persistently holding his lamp, his manservant's eyes also beheld the celestial warriors. The doctrine of Jesus promises that every eye shall see and every tongue confess all that is exposed by the steady holding of the Nazarene's candle toward the universe of God.

Elisha's doctrine reads, "Legions of angels defending the good."

The doctrine of Jesus reads, "The Kingdom of God is come." There is nothing to be created — all is created. There is nothing to be done — all is done.

Your doctrine shines on what is already done and sees nothing but a mass of matter crude, but waiting to be used; or your doctrine shines on the kingdom and shows you a mass of matter and mind crude, but yielding to your orders. You have a mental training which reads, "Thou shalt decree a thing and it shall be established unto thee." So you decree. If your former doctrine read of ugly, hard labor as the lot and law of life, your new doctrine of decree is not yet your hearty doctrine. The labor lamp still sheds its lurid light on the kingdom of God.

If the "decree" doctrine still clings to your mind, the doctrine that "All is finished" is not your light. Decree sheds its electric beams on the kingdom of God at your hand. All is yet artificial, unsatisfactory.

It is easier to "let be" than to decree. And the doctrine of "let be" is the one doctrine that sheds the perfect light on the Kingdom of God here in our broad daylight of our own understanding which we had with the Father before the doctrines of men shed their candles on our mind and invited us to see the kingdom of God from other standpoints than from the light we had and which we were forever.

The letter of Scripture would make me believe that all is darkness in the world and over the world. The letter of Scripture would have me think I had not light of understanding but must get the light from God. The mental of Scripture would make me think that I must speak and think in order to be power and bring forth good.

The spiritual understanding or the God-interpretation would show me that all I have to do is to be. All I have to think is nothing. All I have to speak is nothing. That which was and is and ever will be, cannot be altered by any doctrine I may preach, but my doctrine will cause what is now to show itself as not what is desirable but as that which is heavenly peace and the kingdom that Jesus Christ saw and still sees.

We now know that the right track toward our own smokeless flame of understanding is the only repenting which God knows anything about. If my doctrine turns me toward the flame that cannot be extinguished, which never was extinguished, which will burn forever within my own being, I have repented, that is, turned toward my own God nature. By so doing, I no longer look to another for my information, my inspiration, my happiness. I find all this in myself.

It is the testimony of Jesus Christ that when a man touches right doctrine, he turns with it to look toward his own heart. He does not despise his heart as a physical thing with no reality, he looks toward it as a point of light shining forth from his whole body. He does not despise his heart as a mind center and thus only an instrument to use; he looks toward it as the One only Light. Therein he finds his original form, his first beauty, his undimmed wisdom, his pristine splendor as God. He finds that his own heart is worthy of his whole attention. It is keeping his lamp trimmed and burning for a man to look toward his own heart till he sees within it all that it contains of the God Fire. Then, from that understanding, he is able to shed a light on the heavenly kingdom nigh him which shall not fail.

Jesus Christ received no doctrines from men. He turned Him toward the light that was in Him as in all men before the world was. "I am the Light of the World," was His doctrine when He lost Himself in His own heart flame.

Men of old practiced sitting with their eyes turned toward the heart centers in their own bodies till it exposed the divine prototype of themselves as a being all-glorious. To their first gaze nothing was glorious; to their steady gaze, it became glorious. To their first gaze their own prototype seemed small; to their steady gaze it became mighty and like a devouring flame. Into it all the worlds were able to merge. As Isaiah prophesied, "A little one shall become a thousand and a small one a great nation," and in their Bible they proclaimed, "God is the smallest of the small and the greatest of the great."

As all things far away have the reputation of being small to the eye of sense, so Jesus Christ, the farthest away of all beings according to our sense, seems inconceivably small to that one who thinks of Him as within His own heart. Is not the heart regarded as a small organ performing one of many missions? But what if now the heart is found to be the chief and only organ possessed[11] — so stupendous in its office that when man looks into it, he becomes no longer a man of flesh and bones, but the transcendent Christ. If this doctrine shines with any splendor for you, then one more turn from the literal to the spiritual has been made by you. The heart is God. It contains God.

---

[11] Since the 1980s, the Institute of HeartMath has been discovering that this may, in fact, be the case.

This is a light which Moses said, "Let be." He who understands his own heart, understands God. He who looks out toward the kingdom lying here at our hand from the knowledge which is within his own heart looks from God to God. The true light then shines. He says with Jesus Christ, he says as Jesus Christ, he says it as God — "I am the Light." As God, he says, "I am Understanding." He speaks as God. "Now is come the Kingdom."

"The heart affords a great light," says the Hindu Bible. "It illuminates the senses. In it reside memory, reflection. It is the imperishable one. It is the lamp and center of the body." All Scripture is God. Interpret it as God, and see God.

All your body is God. Interpret it as God, and see it as Spirit unhindered. Nothing clings to Spirit and darkens it.

And all that you have of heart in your religion, so much understanding you have.

According to your heart, you are a seer of God or a seer of not God. Let there be light on this kingdom which lies here at hand. Let many doctrines light as best they may, but only in me can I see it plainly. Let it be plainly visible because my heart is single to one God. The pure in heart shall see it. The understanding heart shall see it. The single eye is my heart.

"The kingdom of god cometh not with observation," said Jesus, but with the knowledge that God is in me, the pure unalterable One.

Whatever doctrine men may turn as lamps on the mighty City we now dwell in the midst of, let me be not deceived into conceiving any doctrine but of the heart.

LESSON IX

Maimonides,[12] who was wise in sacred history, said of the book of Genesis, "Whoever shall find out the true sense of the book of Genesis ought to take care not to divulge it. If a person should discover the true meaning of it by himself or by the aid of another, then he ought to be silent, or if he speak of it, he ought to speak of it but obscurely and in an enigmatical way."

Evidently, Maimonides knew that the book is a parable with a motif. It tells important Spiritual principles in figures of speech. In our day, there are many who doubt entirely that there were ever any such characters as are therein mentioned. It has been called a book written by intuitional memory.

Esdras, [Ezra] a Hebrew priest of 457 B.C., had the experience which mathematicians, musicians and others have sometimes, of suddenly recollecting that what they are doing they have done before, and that there are yet other points about it that they have known. So as from one point to another, they go on making it known to the world, others call them original and wonderful, but they know that they are remembering.

A child one early morning waking tried, with mysterious steps of mind, to remember where that home was from which she had come; but soon the sounds and sights of her earthly and familiar home

---

[12] Maimonides (Rabbi Moses ben Maimon), [A.D. 1135-1204]; Spanish-born Jewish philosopher and still considered among the gr eatest. Author of *The Eight Chapters of Maimonides on Ethics*.

caused her to forget to think of some long past spot and scene. Again, in middle life, came the same experience of trying to remember some wonderful and happy life long gone. So the profound mathematician recollects what once he has known in some other life experience.

Thus Esdras (or Ezra) touched backward upon some points of thought as he had them with the Father before the world was and told his mind's past knowledge in a story. By it, he explained how the Spiritual world is good and uncognizant of matter or evil. He sees the power and splendor of the Spirit of man. He finds it able to multiply and replenish all that its will is set to do. He finds the Spirit of man able to subdue all its world, not by tilling the soil, but by knowledge of Good only.

He finds all the corn and gold created before their shadows or earthly symbols are seen. In the realm of man's Spirit they are not sordid, not scanty nor unreliable, but are good throughout. The good corn never fails. The good gold is never scant. They have knowledge in themselves of how to move into the right places and they have a speech with which to speak to the right people. Their substance is Wisdom. To tell this to the world is to set the fine waves of a new era to flowing through the mind of man.

His spirit is within him and its breath is almighty. As he understands it, he is using his mind to step nearer and nearer to his undying Spirit or Mind that he had in the beginning with the God Mind. When once he touches that Mind, all his ideas of matter, evil, people, events, are changed into the Original Mind. He sees, hears, smells, tastes, feels, as he did at first.

Ezra, the priest (or Esdras, which is the Greek form of the name and when seen must be known as

Ezra), thus touched the unvarnished tops of his own God Mind and forgot matter in Spirit, then saw matter and Adam as shadows flung from the God Mind, as that a man might know what power his own mind had and then imagine what it would be not to have power. By him we see that all the operations through which man now moves himself are his God Mind thinking what it would be not to have power, not to be almighty God.

It is God condescending to be man, condescending to be matter, in a thought, which thought, comprehending the whole of creation as we term it, will remember the God Mind from whence it originated and touch by touch on the harp strings of recollection, will finally touch home again. This thought, comprehending all that is called earthly experience, has taken no time to be thought, though it has put in, as a factor of imagining what it would be to be not powerful, that other ingredient of helpless ignorance, what it would be to be subject to time and change.

"Remember now thy Creator in the days of thy youth." Oh, remember and remember till your mind touches the home point before you have put more time into your imagination! Paul says, "If they had only been mindful of the country from whence they came out." All his own practicing was his trying to be mindful. All the original music, all the brilliant touches of mathematics, or the announcement of mighty truths, are men's recollections step by step backward toward their original knowledge. All the meditations of the adepts of India are their endeavor to recollect.

All the struggle of the thinkers of America are the endeavors of mind to step backward to its home point. The home point is in man. There is nowhere he can go that he is not in his home. The home

Mind is an eternal, absolute point as unkillable as God, because it is of God. And all that he experiences as man, is his thought of what it would be, not to be God.

When he has had enough of such an idea, he may drop it, and what is true may be to him as it was in the beginning, is now, and ever shall be. And what is not true will have no place, as it has none now.

Who has imagined sin, let him know its nature. Who has imagined poverty, let him know its nature. Man is God. Every man is God. What he has chosen to think, was his privilege, his power, his ability. When he chose to imagine matter, he had the right. He had the right even to imagine what it would be to be dust. He had the right to be an idea the whole realm of nature. He had the right to call himself Christ or Adam. He had the right to cease to call himself by any other name than his own name and recollect his majesty and bliss as God. He who learns the art of remembering, will be called a discoverer.

Genius in its splendor is only attention undistracted to one subject till one realization of something unusual is felt, then another realization, then another. He who has learned how to put his mind upon one thing till that thing has revealed the hidden beauty in one new good after another, is practicing memory.

Discovery of Music beyond Beethoven's music will be only the rest of the returning mind on its way of recollecting its God estate.

All the Hindu sacred books were touches of memory. Read their history and see how many of their authors realized that they were not authors but memorizers and how, in order to learn to remember their own Godhood, each mystic learned to remember every statement of God he could gather. He who mixes his imaginations of what it is to be poor, old, sick, feeble, with his statements of God, is like a musician who thinks he must cover himself with pitch and feathers while he is composing. The pitch and feathers distract the attention of his hearers. They take up his own time. They are not necessary. Neither is poverty or pain essential to the religionist's statements of God, but he has distracted himself for ages by making them essential.

God is the undecomposible element, the unmixed principle, the Absolute Knower, whose unchangeable abode is the starting point of man, woman, child, beast, planet, plant, pebble, alike.

It is each one's business to recollect for himself. The pebble can remember as well as Esdras. When you find a piece of gold, it is the gold remembering its first estate and touching you on its home journey. When the bags of gold burst open in Washington it is the first spring of their nature to step out among men in rightful distribution, so realizing one step nearer home.

The stars hear the songs of the men who are now reminding them that all is God. They are gathering up the dropped chords of their ages of time. The sands shine and smile while we repeat the story of the home from whence we came out to imagine what it would be not to be God, They are letting fall their coverings of thought and exposing their glistening hearts. The men of our planet are feeling the springs of the Spirit as we remind ourselves of who we were in the beginning; who we are now, and who we shall be forever. I came forth from God. I know what is not God and what is God. I know now that I am God, and knowing this again, leaving all else, I am in my right Mind.

LESSON X

When mind touches the Absolute it becomes a radiant thing, and men coming in its presence are aware of something out of the ordinary having taken place.

Swedenborg's[13] face shone so after his midnight communings with the Absolute Mind that his servants were frightened. Great miracle workers have overpowered men and women with a nameless power streaming from their presence. They do so in some measure to this day, but as this power seems to leave them when they converse much with men and women or handle material things often, it must be that they approach the Absolute in their praying, for they are not really in touch with it.

All human mind is instrumental. It is not alive. It is not Substance. When it touches the Divine Mind, it is not; this is death. Divine Mind appears; this is Life. As the human mind turns its thoughts and speech upon the Divine Mind, we see a strange shining, we feel a strange power.

Armies always march to victory whose generals touch the Absolute and Eternal Presence while their soldiers sleep.

Mothers who are turning toward the Changeless and Absolute while the waters rage, send ships safely across the stormy waters. Thus it is promised that whatsoever once lays itself on the One Rock of

---

[13] Swedenborg, Emanuel [1688-1722]; Royal engineer of Sweden who, in a series of trances, conversed with angels and became a beloved philosopher and religious writer. He inspired, among many others, Ralph Waldo Emerson and Ernest Holmes.

fire nigh the touch of the thoughts, nigh the touch of the fingers, shall from thenceforth be undefeatable.

Moses spent 30 years in the mountains turning his thoughts entirely upon the everlasting, unquenchable God. His power was then so great that when he lifted his hands for Pharaoh's army to stand back, it came not upon the Israelites. The Red Sea rolled back. The Israelites walked safely over. Moses called that Eternal One, "The Lord." The Absolute Good works and none shall hinder. "Stand ye still and see the salvation. The Lord will fight for you this day."

By whatsoever process you turn the attention of your mind to the Very Present God, it signifies not; you shall touch God by your mind's sight and strike eternal fire for your reward.

There is a practice of breathing seven times deep hoping to touch the Eternal One at the point where the breath leaves off. Many a face glows because the attention has thus been long held toward the Glorious Central God. Many a tongue has startled by its mighty eloquence because the breaths have rolled themselves backward toward the fire point where the Awful Spirit lives and dies not. There, down in the deep bowels shines the fire point. There, back where the minds began, glows the fire point. There, where the breaths extend themselves, blazes the powerful Spirit, So, breathing will lead your mind to the God Mind. Therefore, breathe, ye people, breathe yourselves to death that God may live in you and through you and by you and for you.

"If I make my bed (of attention) in hell, Thou art there. If I ascend up into heaven, Thou art there." [Psalm 139:8] It is to be born of God that the human mind travails.

"Greater love hath no man than this, that a man lay down his life for his friend." Lay down attentions earthward by breathing till you die, that your only Friend, the Lord Jehovah, in whom is everlasting Strength, may live in your place. There is a practice of finding the strings of light that stretch through the airs by giving over, touching and testing all things eternal, that the strings that bind the atoms together may harmonize and vibrate with our attention till touch and taste are dead that the strings divine may live and be our visible life. This is the Soul string like a harp anew and the face glistens like the transfigured man on Mt. Hermon.

"I drew them with the bands of love and they knew not that I healed them."

Touch the strings of light with your attention toward them till you are dead, that they may live in your place. For they are the radiant beams that shine straight from the Absolute God. Laying your whole being on their strong pinions, you are borne to your shining heaven. You are one with God. "The Father and I are One."

There is nothing the wandering attentions of mind are struggling after but to see the Absolute. "The Son can do nothing only what He seeth the Father do."

The struggling of the instrument is to be alive through death. It longs for the Absolute and Eternal One. It would see that which it cannot and live. None may look upon the Absolute and live. At one supreme moment, taught the Hindus of old, by any process, all acts are abandoned and the heart takes sanctuary with the Absolute. One is that One and nothing less than that One.

"Abandoning all acts, take sanctuary with Me alone. I shall liberate thee from all sins, do thou not grieve."

If a man try the practice of putting his thoughts to one theme alone, there shall come a supreme moment when he understands that one theme. He is It. Then must the theme die in It. That which is Holy Fire in the theme to which a mind has set itself shall live. That which is Holy Fire has burned the rest away. That mind that sets itself to some divine word with some divine meaning must be burned by the meaning of the word till only that which is undying, indestructible Substance is left.

The word God will thus operate. The name Jesus Christ will thus operate. The words, "I am I," will thus operate.

At one moment, the uttermost power of the word is reached. All is dead but it. Thus even the brooks are running to death that only the undying and changeless water of life may be visible. The dry sands disappear that only the Spirit may be visible. The fires are burning to death that the deathless fires of One may be seen. The mind of man hastes that it may die for the Absolute Mind to be left. He to whom all the actions of nature are the visible hastening of all things into dissolvable walls, is aware that himself is something at his central point that is undissolviable. He sees that all things have also their undissolvable center point. The undying spirit of the water brook, the undying substance of the fire, the deathless center of the wind, are all one center.

This knowledge fixes the attention of Mind on Mind, the individual on the undividable. (The individual is the undividable.) Mind is thereby aware that there is one alone — that itself is that One.

As one shakes himself on awakening from slumber, so Mind arouses itself, and its electric fires illuminate Omnipresence. There is nothing but the God Mind. Wherever you look, it is God Center that attracts you. Knowing these two truths, viz., that each center is the God that attracts you, and that it is your own God center that is attracted — you know all that is to be known.

That which seems to be matter is gone by this knowledge. That which seems to be evil is gone by this knowledge. That which seems to be ignorance is gone by this knowledge. That which has been written of knowledge, comes thus to pass. "Ye shall know the truth and the truth shall make you free."

The only truth to know of matter is that it is not, for Spirit is all. "I choose to know Spirit rather than to imagine matter," said Spinoza. The whole realm of matter is supposition. Suppose your house should burn? What would you do?

Suppose you were Spirit, free and wise, and should for one instant imagine yourself bound in matter? What would you do? Suppose you, as-free Spirit, were to forget your own free nature? Suppose you saw all the realm of God as bound in flesh? Suppose you saw all the free Spirit of the universe as a mass of ignorance needing instructions, would all your supposings make the facts of the case any different? The choice to know or to suppose is mine and yours. Covering myself with suppositions, I experience earthly conditions. Uncovering my original knowledge, I shine over and transform all things.

At my undefeatable point, I am the Absolute. When I spend the night watches attending to the undefeatable Absolute in the universe, I am laying aside suppositions. I am showing myself. It is no wonder that miracles are wrought by those who know how, by any process whatsoever, to lay off suppositions and strike back upon knowledge.

LESSON XI

If one is born blind or made blind by accident, he educates his fingers to be eyes for him. If one is born deaf, he educates his skin and muscles, his bones and nerves to be ears.

The brain is said to hold in its convolutions, a gentle gray matter, a slight agitation of which causes to spring forth the speech and actions of a man. If a large brain has small quantum of gray matter, the man is not intelligent. If a small brain has large store of gray matter, the man is wise. If the fingers and toes of blind people are investigated, it is observed that the brain has transferred some of its gray matter to them, that intelligence may be active through them. The brain by this generous giving declares to all mankind that intelligence dwells not in the brain only, nor is dependent upon brain, but is shed and spread abroad wheresoever it lists to generate gray matter.

Plainly then, gray matter itself is subservient to intelligence and is generated or not generated according to intelligence. It cannot distribute or renew itself. Thus, intelligence is master and ruler of the fine etheric substance which acts as intelligence but is naught but an instrument.

It is a great marvel that men have concerned themselves so much with the instruments they use, and so little with the maker of these instruments; for it is clearly to be seen that the maker of an instrument must know how to multiply and replenish it many times over, and if a man could get into the good graces of the Intelligence that forms and manages gray matter, he might get the favor of the marvelous storage thereof and bring forward to the attention of his race, some undreamed-of powers, inventions, helps.

It is evident that the gray matter is but an instrument in some mysterious being's hands. While the scholars in our schools have intensely concerned themselves with this instrument, its maker has been little or not at all regarded. The Hindus have taught for thousands of years that there is a luminous spot in the brain which, being watched steadfastly by the mental eyes, will give one the power to see divine beings. They have taught that as the physical body is warmed, invigorated, strengthened by the sun, so this luminous governor of the head and body is renewed and strengthened by some mighty Spiritual Sun unseen by the eyes of man, unheard by his ears, untouched by his fingers. Only the luminous spot in the brain can see the Spiritual Sun, can feel its warmth, can move in its smile. This luminous spot is the maker of the gray matter. If the luminous governor thereof receives but little light from the Spiritual Sun, it casts but little shade of itself in gray matter, and gray matter being absent, there is then but little man, but little character, but little worth.

The maker of a shadow is the substance that casts it. The substance may stand right in the midst of the shadow. When the sunshine is great enough, the shadow is gone, then the substance is alone in the light. If the luminous spot in the brain is the substance that casts the shade men call gray, matter, when it is all shone upon from every direction by the Spiritual Sun, then there cannot be any more gray matter, there cannot be any more flesh man, great or small character, worthy or unworthy will, or sense.

The luminous substance is then all Spiritual Sun. The Spiritual Sun is all there is. As the shadow disappears when it looks toward it so flesh man with his senses disappears when he looks toward gray matter, his governor. So gray matter disappears when it looks toward the luminous spot, its governor; so the luminous spot disappears when it looks toward the Spiritual Sun, its governor; so the Spiritual Sun disappears when it looks toward the Supreme unnamed Origin of all, the One Starting Point of all that moves or stands still.

If the flesh, is under the governorship of gray matter and gray matter under the governorship of the luminous spot, and the luminous spot is under the governorship of the Spiritual Sun, and the Spiritual Sun is under the governorship of the unnamed Origin, the Starting Point of all, it is the business of man's whole being to look utterly away toward the Starting Point of all that is. That Starting Point is the Substance that casts the shadows which we give so many names to. Its only name is the One undescribed Mind. All other mind is but supposition. It is plain that all other mind but It, is supposition; for everything that all other mind tells its body or its senses to do is an experiment with both itself and its agent.

Does the musician positively know that his fingers will perform with him at the concert hall tonight? Does he positively know his head will keep level and not get rattled? Does the forensic orator positively know that his thoughts will charm and chain and magnetize his audience this night? Not even the most brilliant mathematician is positive he will not blunder. All is supposition, and vanishes from the memory of the most enrapt listener and observer, so that not an item thereof will remain after a certain lapse of days.

There is a new tide of thought springing forth from man's late discovery that the suppositional life is not worth living. "What is the life that is worth while? cries man.

Listen: "I am, and there is none beside me." This is the word that streams from the One at the Starting Point.

> "Nature is the picture of your thoughts which Thou hast suppressed. Thou hast not known Me. Thou hast supposed something not Me.
>
> "Nature has no actuality. Thou art Nature's painter. On the plastic clouds of nothing nature Thou hast laid your suppositions, and behold trees and rocks and stars. What an artist you can be! Your picture shall all be resolved back into nothingness when you look toward Me.
>
> "When you speak well of My Goodness and majesty, Thou art Jesus Christ.
>
> "When you no longer speak well of My majesty and goodness, but see Me as I am. Thou hast a Science higher than the word. Jesus Christ is the. word of majesty and goodness. Jesus Christ gives up the keys of the word of good and truth when He no longer has to speak truth. He is free from the word."

The giving up of even the noblest figures impressed on the walls of existence is Jesus Christ giving up His words. The Jesus Christ Mind sees goodness, majesty, loveliness. Then when goodness, majesty, loveliness, have wrought their highest mission, they also cease and that which is independent of all states appears.

The air around men is filled with divine aroma. This is the eternal splendor which he who knows how to find lose himself as he finds it. He breathes the breath thereof and becomes the living Man, Soul, God. He becomes the aroma. It is the all-present, all-pervading Wisdom. It is the breath which the ancients knew would make man God if he breathed, the One Wonderful Presence of whom all things else are shadows. The One Intelligence of whom all other intelligences are suppositions — the One Word, the One Name, that fills the universe, of whom all names are symbols.

The Science of the word as Jesus Christ is the Science of Good and Truth, but the Science that Jesus Christ knows as He gives up the Science of Good and Truth is the Science of the Unspoken Word, the One Name that fills the 'universe, of whom even Good and Truth are but symbols.

This is the One Substance, the One Intelligence, that governs all things. It is the Eternal Refuge, the Everlasting God, The Absolute Wisdom, the glorious Intelligence everywhere One.

Whatsoever is not This, is not at all.

LESSON XII

The two ideas, "Use" and "Theory," have their adherents among mankind. These adherents despise each other for their idea, not despising their Soul per se.

When we are beloved, we are beloved for our ideas consciously or unconsciously held. When we are disliked, we are disliked for our ideas consciously or unconsciously held. This plane of loving and not loving is the plane of ideas and their demonstrations.

Usefulness is demonstration. An idea not yet worked out into practice is theory. When it is worked out into blood and bones it is usefulness.

The adherents of blood and bones twit the adherents of theories with not living the life. The adherents of theories twit the adherents of bones and blood with living the life too much in the material.

A man may say that a statement is not worth anything till it is made into good eyes and oatmeal. A man may say that a statement is adorable truth whether it has cured your eyes or not; whether it has furnished Coxey's army[14] with oatmeal or not. These men both rejoice when a $100 bill arrives in their hands as the usefulness of their theories. They would not say a word about anything without such self-conviction that they would be satisfied in what they are unclothed of (greenbacks and ideas) if they were utterly free.

The Indian tomahawks his neighbor Indian to get his wampum. The Yankee tomahawks his neighbor Yankee to get his greenbacks. The Relig-

---

[14] Coxey's Army was a protest march by unemployed workers from the United States, led by the populist Jacob Coxey. They marched on Washington D.C. in 1894.

ionist tomahawks his neighbor religionist to get his ideas. The only difference between the religionist and the Indian is that the Indian will hug and kiss and love the captured wampum, while the religionist will strike and crush the captured idea.

Whoever standing calmly and coolly by the battle of uses and theories and touches them not, but utterly detached from either money, wampum, religious principle or men who wrangle, knows them for what they are and knows himself as free from either, knows himself as he is — he only is secure.

Security is the aim of the adherents of theories. Security is the aim of the adherents of uses. Security means out of reach of vanquishment, out of reach of necessity, out of reach of contention, out of reach of effort.

The doctrine of Jesus Christ is entirely of security. The "secure man" was His theme. His Name is God-man. He is the Father and the Father is He. That is, He is that secure First Mind that is not entangled with wampum, oatmeal, money or religious ideas. The Brahmin religions said He is the unattached One, but the Secure One will not be reached by tomahawking bodies or tomahawking religions. Ages of tomahawks have proved this proclamation.

The Secure One is that one who is reached by leaving principle of adherence and being no adherent. All the adhering tendency being dropped, I am unburdened sufficiently to turn about and face my Secure Self. That Secure Self is the One that the prophets, the priests, the millionaires, the Czars, the mayors, the operators, are squabbling to be.

> Oh, Thou, Mighty One! I see that Thou art not reached by effort. Thou art reached by facing Thee, released from efforts.
>
> Thou needest not to toil and moil. You need not to use wampum. Thou needest not to use money. Thou

needest not to use religion. Thou needest not to be praised. Thou needest not to be watching out for the main chances to cut thy way through squabbling money grabbers or squabbling religionists. Thou needest not to make thy living. Thou hast no debts to pay. Thou hast no position to hold. Thou hast nothing to hold. Thou needest nothing.

Wonderful One! How easy it is to envy Thee. This is the envy that reaches security. Thy unweighted, unattached indifference — I, by envying, become secure.

Thou art the One of whom I am jealous, for Thou sittest on that throne I have been squabbling with ideas and hands to secure. This is the jealousy that reaches security, for it keeps me watching Thee; and watching Thee, I secure Thee. I am Thee.

If Thou hast that security from struggle, that security from fear, that security from danger, that security from money, that security from religion, that the Czars and the ministers are hating each other in order to capture, how can I help hating Thee. This is the malice which reaches security, for it keeps me watching Thee. Anything that keeps me watching Thee is a freeing from adherencies. It is a sight of security to watch Thee, though I watch Thee by fighting Thee, for it makes me forget wampum and money and people and religion. I remember only Thee.

I see Thee while I fight Thee, and I remember this is Jesus Christ taking the Kingdom by force. "The Kingdom of Heaven suffereth violence and the violent take it by force."

I, like Jacob, fight Thee for Thy security. Give it to me. "I will not let Thee go except Thou bless me." If I have contention, it shall be with Thee. What is squabbling man that should contend with him for that which he has not? Thou hast what I have panted after since time was.

To look toward Thee is to secure Thy security. Hast Thou not always spoken, "Turn unto Me"? See! I wrestle with Thee, Thou Secure One. I am after all that Thou art and have. I will not let Thee go except Thou give me Thyself.

WISEWOMAN PRESS

Books by Emma Curtis Hopkins

- *Class Lessons of 1888 (WiseWoman Press)*
- *Bible Interpretations (WiseWoman Press)*
- *Esoteric Philosophy in Spiritual Science (WiseWoman Press)*
- *Genesis Series 1894 (WiseWoman Press)*
- *High Mysticism (WiseWoman Press)*
- *Self Treatments with Radiant I Am (WiseWoman Press)*
- *The Gospel Series (WiseWoman Press)*
- *Judgment Series in Spiritual Science (WiseWoman Press)*
- *Drops of Gold (WiseWoman Press)*
- *Resume (WiseWoman Press)*
- *Scientific Christian Mental Practice (DeVorss)*

Books about Emma Curtis Hopkins and her teachings

- *Emma Curtis Hopkins, Forgotten Founder of New Thought* – Gail Harley
- *Unveiling Your Hidden Power: Emma Curtis Hopkins' Metaphysics for the 21st Century (also as a Workbook and as A Guide for Teachers)* – Ruth L. Miller
- *Power to Heal: Easy reading biography for all ages* – Ruth Miller

To find more of Emma's work, including some previously unpublished material, log on to:

www.highwatch.org

www.emmacurtishopkins.com

To order go to our website
www.wisewomanpress.com

WISEWOMAN PRESS

Vancouver, WA 98665
800.603.3005
www.wisewomanpress.com

Books by Emma Curtis Hopkins

- *Resume*
- *The Gospel Series*
- *Class Lessons of 1888*
- *Self Treatments including Radiant I Am*
- *High Mysticism*
- *Genesis Series 1894*
- *Esoteric Philosophy in Spiritual Science*
- *Drops of Gold Journal*
- *Judgment Series*
- *Bible Interpretations: Series I, thru XXII*

Books by Ruth L. Miller

- *Unveiling Your Hidden Power: Emma Curtis Hopkins' Metaphysics for the 21st Century*
- *Coming into Freedom: Emily Cady's Lessons in Truth for the 21st Century*
- *150 Years of Healing: The Founders and Science of New Thought*
- *Power Beyond Magic: Ernest Holmes Biography*
- *Power to Heal: Emma Curtis Hopkins Biography*
- *The Power of Unity: Charles Fillmore Biography*
- *Power of Thought: Phineas P. Quimby Biography*
- *The Power of Insight: Thomas Troward Biography*
- *The Power of the Self: Ralph Waldo Emerson Biography*
- *Uncommon Prayer*
- *Spiritual Success*
- *Finding the Path*

Books by Ute Maria Cedilla

- *The Mysticism of Emma Curtis Hopkins*
- *Volume 1 Finding the Christ*
- *Volume 2 Ministry: Realizing The Christ One in All*

www.ingramcontent.com/pod-product-compliance
Lightning Source LLC
Chambersburg PA
CBHW060420090426
42734CB00011B/2390